Spirits
of Georgia's
Southern Crescent

Christina A. Barber

4880 Lower Valley Road, Atglen, Pennsylvania 19310

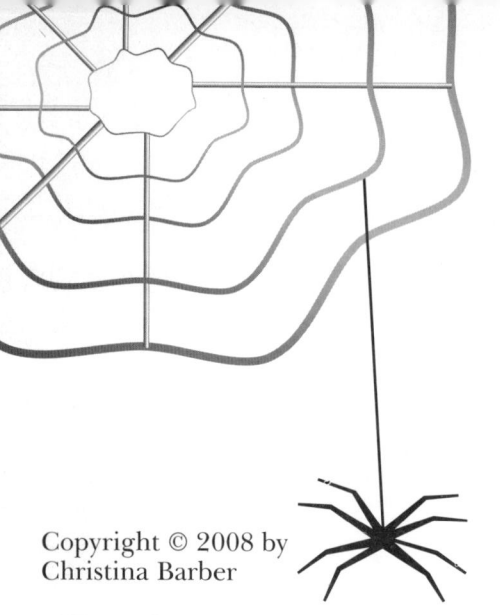

Library of Congress Control Number:
2008925107

Designed by Stephanie Daugherty
Type set in A Charming Font Expanded/
NewBskvll BT

ISBN: 978-0-7643-2945-6

Printed in China

Schiffer Books are available at special
discounts for bulk purchases for sales
promotions or premiums. Special
editions, including personalized
covers, corporate imprints, and
excerpts can be created in large
quantities for special needs. For more
information contact the publisher:

Schiffer Publishing Ltd.
4880 Lower Valley Road
Atglen, PA 19310
Phone: (610) 593-1777
Fax: (610) 593-2002
E-mail: Info@schifferbooks.com

Please visit our web site catalog at
www.schifferbooks.com

We are always looking for people to
write books on new and related subjects.
If you have an idea for a book, please
contact us at the above address.

This book may be purchased from the
publisher. Include $5.00 for shipping.
Please try your bookstore first. You may
write for a free catalog.

In Europe, Schiffer books are
distributed by:
Bushwood Books
6 Marksbury Ave.
Kew Gardens
Surrey TW9 4JF
England
Phone: 44 (0)208 392-8585
Fax: 44 (0)208 392-9876
E-mail: Info@bushwoodbooks.co.uk
Website: www.bushwoodbooks.co.uk

Free postage in the UK. Europe: air
mail at cost. Try your bookstore first.

Dedication

This book is dedicated to my family. Your patience and love is greatly appreciated, especially when my writing projects take me away from precious time with you. And while I'm a master of words, I can only think of two which fit. Thank you.

Acknowledgements

To my family — Your undying support and love keeps me moving.

To Joey Ward and The West Georgia Paranormal Research Society — Thank you for sharing your knowledge and discussing 'ghostly' theories with me over pizza (make mine onion!). Visit the West Georgia Paranormal Research Society with your questions at www.wgprs.com.

To Chester County Paranormal Research Society in Pennsylvania for use of their Glossary. Please visit www.ChesterCountyprs.com for more information.

To Elizabeth Beers — Thank you for sharing your historical knowledge of Coweta with me.

To The Male Academy Museum — Thank you for allowing me to peruse your extensive historical collection.

To Scott Lefebvre for allowing me to use his Guide for Urban Exploration.

Thanks to Forrest Schultz for helping to secure some stories, as well as all your help getting the word out about this book.

To the wonderful folks at Wolf Camera in Newnan. A huge thank you for helping with the photos and assisting this fledgling photographer.

To all those named and unnamed — A huge *Thanks* for sharing your stories. Without you, this book wouldn't be possible.

Contents

Introduction

U ndoubtedly you've picked up this book because you are interested in ghosts and paranormal activity. While many people speculate answers about ghosts, always remember there is no true expert. We can only observe, investigate, and continue to pursue answers to our ever-growing list of questions.

I've thoroughly researched the subject, attended investigations with ghost hunting groups, and asked more than my share of questions.

The role of a paranormal investigator is not to fabricate tales or doctor evidence. A true investigator looks for real facts and debunks myths. They perform their work as scientists — to seek answers and to prove, or disprove, theory. If you are interested in learning more, I encourage you to seek out groups of investigators in your area.

A Story For Everyone!

One thing I've discovered over the years, is that everyone has a ghost story. Some people are more willing to discuss their experiences, while others find it easier to forget or deny what they've seen or heard. And what campout wouldn't be complete with the scary fireside tales? Many children can recall at least one ghostly tale which was told to them beside the glowing embers.

One question that I'm frequently asked is, "Have you ever seen a ghost?" That question is a very difficult one to answer. 'Seen' is a very subjective word in ghost hunting circles. The word seen, in most cases, refers to a Full-Bodied Apparition — what most people would think of when you say ghost — that hazy, transparent image of a person. An FBA (full-bodied apparition) is very rare and I've not had the pleasure of spotting such an entity. However, I have had other experiences which I will share throughout the book.

While public interest in ghosts is growing, as evidenced by television shows and articles, I understand the hesitancy of people to claim they've experienced paranormal activity or that they live in a haunted house. Many fear ridicule. Others know it could cost them their jobs or social standing within the community or church. Georgia is in the Bible Belt, where church greatly influences the lives of all. With that in mind, I've kept the anonymity of some of my sources at their request.

Every one of the stories contained in this book came from a first-hand experience. The person or persons who experienced or witnessed the paranormal activity told their story directly to me. Each and every story is amazing and true. Many stories also have supporting evidence from investigation teams.

I hope you enjoy the ghostly tour of The Southern Crescent, Georgia!

Chapter 1

Coweta County — A Brief History

Old Courthouse, Newnan Square

C oweta County, Georgia is located in the southwestern part of the state, forty minutes from the metropolis of Atlanta. The entire county is approximately 443 square miles or 284,000 acres in size.

A French Map from 1733 titles the territory as Caouita, thusly named for the residents, the Coweta Indians. Subsequent maps also call the land Couita

or Kawita. The Coweta Indians were the second great Muskogee tribe of the lower Creek Indians. Their Chief was William McIntosh.

Purchasing the land from the Creek Indians in 1825, the State Legislature established it as Coweta County. In 1828, Newnan became the county seat.

In 1850, the town square consisted of wooden shacks. Coweta had rich soil and cotton farming was the main stay of life. To house the goods, the first cotton warehouse was built in 1852. The growing cotton industry allowed for Newnan to attract interests from the railroad. The passenger railroad line opened in 1851.

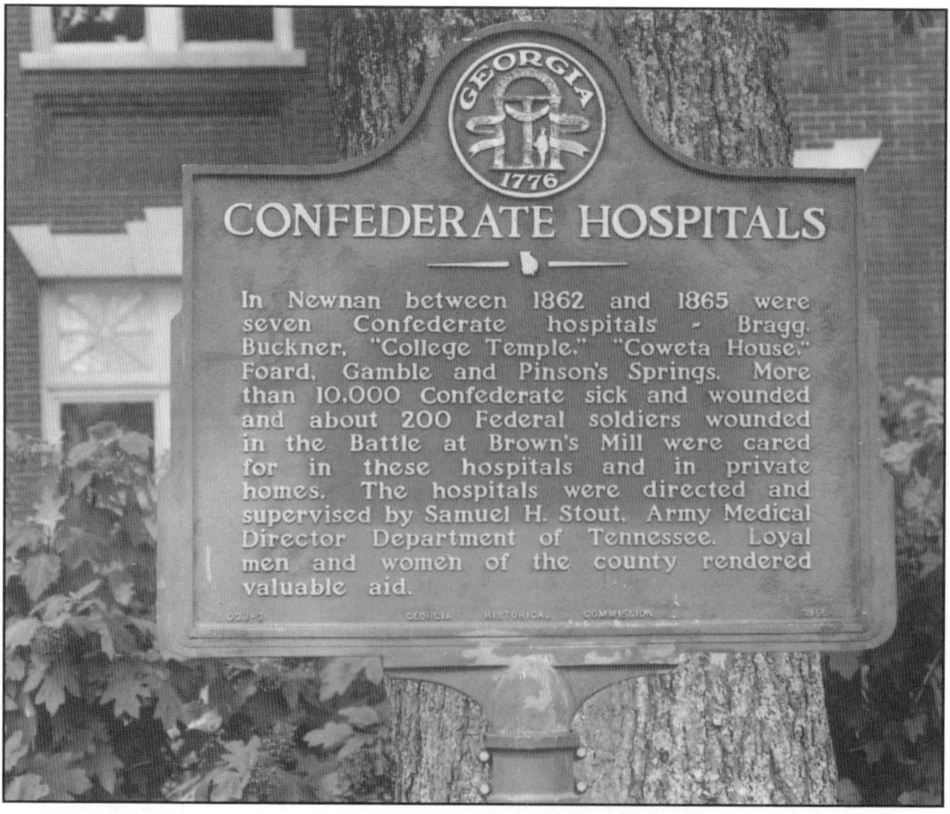

Confederate Hospital historical marker, Court Square, Newnan.

Historical marker.

During the Civil War, Newnan became a hospital town because of its access to the railroad and distance from the fighting. Originally planned to house five to six hundred injured, Newnan soon became overwhelmed with over ten thousand ill or wounded Confederate soldiers. Hotels, businesses, churches, and the town square became makeshift hospital quarters to accommodate the injured. Sheds made from tent cloth and board sides were erected around the town square to serve the many wounded. Plantation owners contributed vegetables and other crops to help the soldiers and their families.

In 1864, the Civil War came to Newnan; the Battle of Browns Mill took place only three miles south of town. Union General E. M. McCook's forces attacked the small Confederate army lead by General Joseph Wheeler. McCook's army was deftly defeated by Wheeler's cavalry troops, a complete surprise to McCook.

Confederate grave marker.

Oak Hill Cemetery, Newnan.

Confederate graves, Oak Hill Cemetery, Newnan.

Newnan finally recovered from the effects of the War by 1875. By 1900, textiles were the primary source of income for most residents of Coweta County. Cotton growing, selling, and manufacturing allowed for electricity, sewers, and paved streets.

Today, many of the historic homes and businesses still line the streets. These beautiful buildings depict an unsettled time from our Country's history. Yet these grand structures remain steadfast, unyielding to the modern era.

Chapter 2

The Tale of Baker Bob

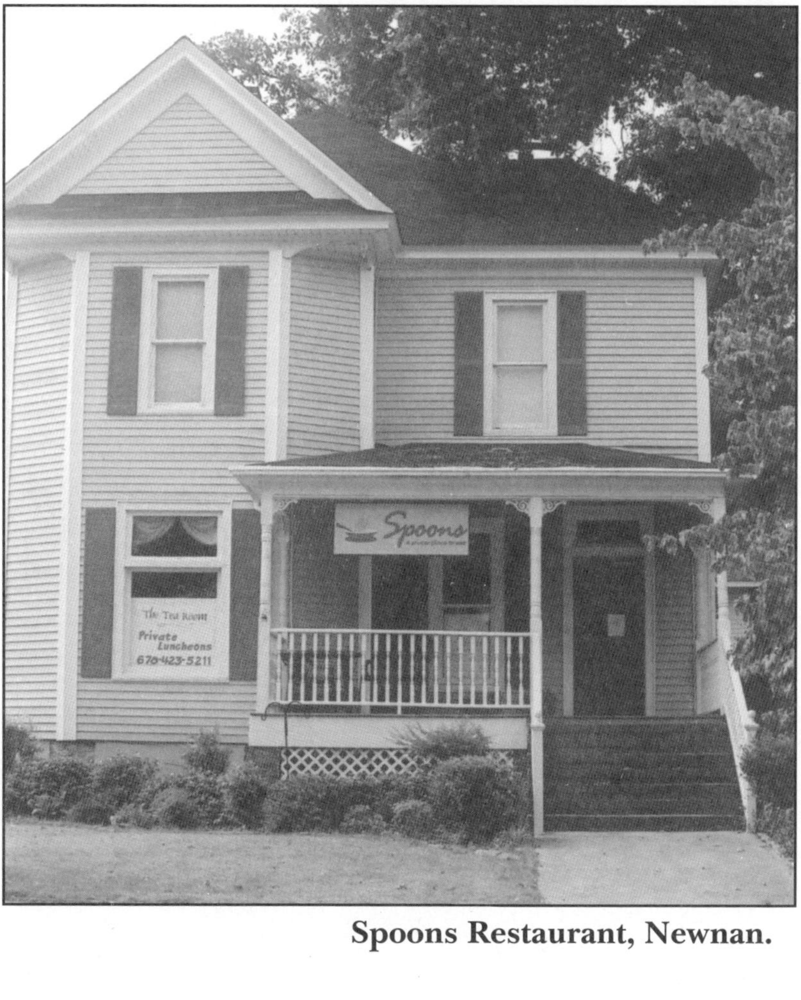

Spoons Restaurant, Newnan.

Spoons Restaurant
24 West Broad Street
Newnan, Georgia
Telephone: 678-423-5211

Spoons Restaurant is one of my favorite establishments here in Newnan. They have a great lunch menu, a lovely atmosphere, and an extremely active and unique entity. Settling in with a great cup of soup and a salad, I began to listen to the tales of 'Baker Bob' as told by the owners, Carol and Debbie. These ladies are no shrinking violets and have numerous hair-raising, intriguing stories about their house.

Built in 1898, the home had played host to various inhabitants. It had been a Parsonage for the First Methodist Church, a residence for a local baker, and an antique shop, gift shop, as well as a home to many renters over the years.

It All Comes Down to Fate…and Renovations!

Fate seemed to guide Debbie and Carol to this house. The owner had recently placed it on the market, but had stated it was 'one renter away from demolition.' Regardless, the ladies saw the potential for something special, and purchased the house. Debbie recalls that the house was dark and sad looking, in desperate need of repairs and love.

Shortly after the purchase, they began the renovation process. Carpenters, plumbers, and electricians were called upon to undertake this huge project.

Soon the new owners began to receive reports from the workers that items would disappear. Tape measures, keys, hammers had simply vanished. The ladies dismissed it without a thought. Of course, the items would reappear again, but in rather unusual places, and often days later.

Come On In—or Not!

A burly mechanic was replacing Freon for one of their refrigerated storage cases. It was after regular business hours, and he was alone in the house. He needed supplies from his home, and had telephoned his wife to bring over a special grade of coolant. He heard the bell on the front door ring and the door slam, indicating that someone had arrived.

Expecting his wife, he called out, "I'm back here, honey."

Moments passed, yet she hadn't come over to him. He called again with the same result. Saying that he felt the hair on the back of his neck rise, he decided to go see who had come through the door. When he arrived at the front door, he saw that it was still firmly locked, but the bell at the top of the door swung back and forth. He left telling Debbie and Carol that he wouldn't return unless someone else was present.

Cleanliness is Next to Ghostliness

The cleaning lady told the restaurateurs that she would no longer clean the house, if she were alone. Concerned, the ladies inquired about her reason. The woman explained that while she was alone in the house sweeping the floor, the back of her blouse rose up and icy fingers touched her.

The Police Are Always Welcome...

About two weeks before opening day, the ladies sat in the kitchen after a long day trying to work out the new menu. While the renovations were moving along, they still had no telephone service. A loud knock on the front door, accompanied by a man's voice echoed through the house.

"NPD," interrupted their conversation.

They answered the door, to find a policeman and four other police cars at the house.

He explained that someone from their address had called 911. Very confused the ladies tried to assure the officer that nothing was wrong. However, he seemed to think the ladies were in horrible trouble and insisted on checking the property. Of course they agreed. They then explained that they didn't have telephone service yet.

After a thorough search and an embarrassing evening, Debbie and Carol stood on the front porch waving goodbye to the police. Neither could explain how it could have happened.

Moving...and All the Ghostly Events that Come With it!

Finally, moving day! However, the happy occasion was interrupted by another visit by our ghostly entity. Carol would be living upstairs, while maintaining the restaurant downstairs. On the evening of the move into the building, Debbie received a call at home from Carol. "I don't know if I'm going to be able to stay here tonight," were Carol's words.

She had heard sounds in the attic like someone was moving heavy furniture around. Carol didn't spend her first night in the new house. Perhaps 'Bob' was simply adjusting to his new house mate.

Days after opening, Debbie's mother was visiting. She used the ladies room which is located under the staircase. When she came out, she insisted she had heard someone running down the stairs and out the front door, slamming the door on their way out. No one had left the building,

much less run down the stairs. This scene has played out more than a dozen times for customers and other family members alike.

Carol also told me about the time she heard a loud crash downstairs while she was upstairs. She cautiously descended the steps, not certain if a thief prowled the property. When she walked into the main room and turned on the light, she noticed the top to the large tea decanters was on the ground.

Electrical and Ringing Ghosts

Debbie and Carol both said that their ghost loves to play with electricity. Sometimes he will cause an outage in half the room, while the other half functions properly. They've checked the fuse box, even had an electrician inspect the wiring. All appears normal.

Another common prank 'Baker Bob' likes to play involves the telephone. He has caused the telephone to ring, yet when the receiver is picked up and the call answered, the telephone continues to ring. Once, it rang in a steady tone for about three minutes. They have changed telephones, changed service providers, to no avail. Customers have even witnessed the strange telephone calls.

Another telephone incident involved Debbie's cell phone calling the restaurant and leaving her cell phone's voicemail message on the restaurant's answering machine.

What's In a Name?

'Baker Bob' got his name from Carol who explains it as, "Well, he messes with my stuff in the kitchen. So, we named him *Baker Bob*."

She goes on to tell about how she'll have extreme difficulty cooking a roast. Carol and Debbie say that half of the roast will be fully cooked, at 160 degrees, while the other half is raw.

Baker Bob also likes to play with the pilot light on the stove. Carol noticed that one unit was out, and did not have the time to relight it.

She said, "Bob, you want to do something useful? How about lighting the pilot light for me?"

She exited the room, and when she returned the light was lit. This has happened on numerous occasions.

One afternoon when Rose, an employee, and Debbie talked, a ladle floated between the two and then suddenly dropped to the floor. Both continued the conversation ignoring the attempt to attract their attention.

One Ghost Handled!

But that is how Carol and Debbie handle their ghost; they simply ignore his pranks. Regardless of his attempts to unsettle the duo, they remain steadfast and committed to the house and business.

One very interesting fact of note is that Bob doesn't seem to have a particular time of day which he prefers to do his mischief. He has shown up day and night, and even when the customers are in the restaurant at lunchtime.

Another important fact about the ethereal spirit is that any attempts of photography in the main room adjacent to the kitchen reveal a bright blur of light and distortion in the photo. No one is certain who the spirit is that inhabits the house on West Broad Street, but they all agree that Baker Bob is a harmless entity. Many neighbors have suggested an

exorcism to rid the house of the spirit. But Debbie and Carol have become accustomed to sharing their life with a ghost.

I noted that all the while during our chat, nothing unusual took place. However, I have to say that the temperature seemed on the cold side of normal. Not having any instruments to measure temperature, I couldn't prove if it were just my imagination or if Baker Bob stood in the room, listening them tell all of his tales.

Further Investigation…or A Cold Encounter

On a return visit to the restaurant for an investigation, an isolated cold spot followed me. It started in the main dining room and situated itself around my neck and chest area. I moved around slowly attempting to locate a draft or other reason for the icy chill. I waved my hands around my body pinpointing the exact location and found the spot was isolated to the area around me. As I moved between rooms, so did the cold spot.

West Georgia Paranormal Research Society also visited, although they did not find any conclusive evidence. However, they did feel that there was activity in the house that merited additional investigation.

Chapter 3

A True Gentleman Ghost

Ten East Washington restaurant, front porch, Newnan.

Ten East Washington
10 East Washington Street
Newnan, Georgia
Telephone: 770-502-9100

I spent part of an afternoon talking with Chef George Rasovsky at his restaurant located at Ten East Washington Street. He steadily worked in his kitchen while we chatted about the ghost.

George told me that anyone who is sensitive to paranormal energy can always feel something in the building. He said they will notice something immediately. "They always ask me, do you have a ghost? When I say yes, they tell me they knew it and could feel him."

George tells me he knows his ghost is a *him*, because of an event witnessed by a previous employee. Eleven years ago, a female employee told George she saw a man standing behind her while she looked into the mirror in the hallway. She said she saw him standing behind her, and when she turned around there was no one there—yet she saw him very clearly in the reflection of the mirror. It scared her at the time.

This male ghost is also a gentleman. George said that many times he'll be trying to go out the front door, but his hands are full. The door will open for him and close once he's outside. Apparently, this helpful apparition has also opened the door in the same manner for customers.

The ghost at Ten East Washington will also turn on the coffee maker. George says that he'll walk into the kitchen and the coffee is brewing — and there's no timer on that coffee machine. Occasionally, glasses would tumble off the bar area. Luckily, none of those glasses have ever broken.

George said, "He's a good spirit here. He's never done anything bad or done any harm."

Chef George is very relaxed and casual about having a ghost in his building. He's even said that he hasn't noticed any activity lately. However, he believes that may be just because he's become accustomed to working and living with a ghost.

History and Renovations

Built in 1895 as a private residence, Ten East Washington was the very first house on the street. A few years later, they built a building directly next door, with barely a breezeway between the structures.

Ten East Washington had once been a doctor's office, then, according to George, it became a pizza restaurant. After the pizza restaurant closed, it became a fine-dining establishment, similar to George's restaurant. But that business only lasted about three years. The building then sat vacant for two years before George moved in around 1995.

Once George started renovations, he noticed signs of paranormal activity. He said things would fall. Items would be misplaced.

George recently purchased an adjacent building and created a larger facility for private parties. I inquired about any activity in the second building. An open doorway connects both buildings, which they built to have easy access. He told me the only place anyone experienced anything was in the main building, not in the new addition.

Chef George has not had a professional team of paranormal investigators come to his restaurant. He is curious, however, at what they could possibly find.

Further Investigation

When I arrived at Ten East, I removed my digital voice recorder from my bag and fiddled around with the settings. However, when I looked at the power level indicator, I noticed it was very low, almost out. The batteries were brand new, just replaced. I removed them, replaced them with another set of batteries, and interviewed Chef George.

However, when I returned home, I pulled out the set of old batteries and placed them into the recorder — it was a nearly full charge.

I know ghosts can drain batteries, which is why I always carry a few sets of backups. Now, I'm fairly certain that George and I weren't alone during our conversation. I believe we had a ghostly visitor listening in on the discussion the entire time.

Chapter 4

You'd Better Believe in Me

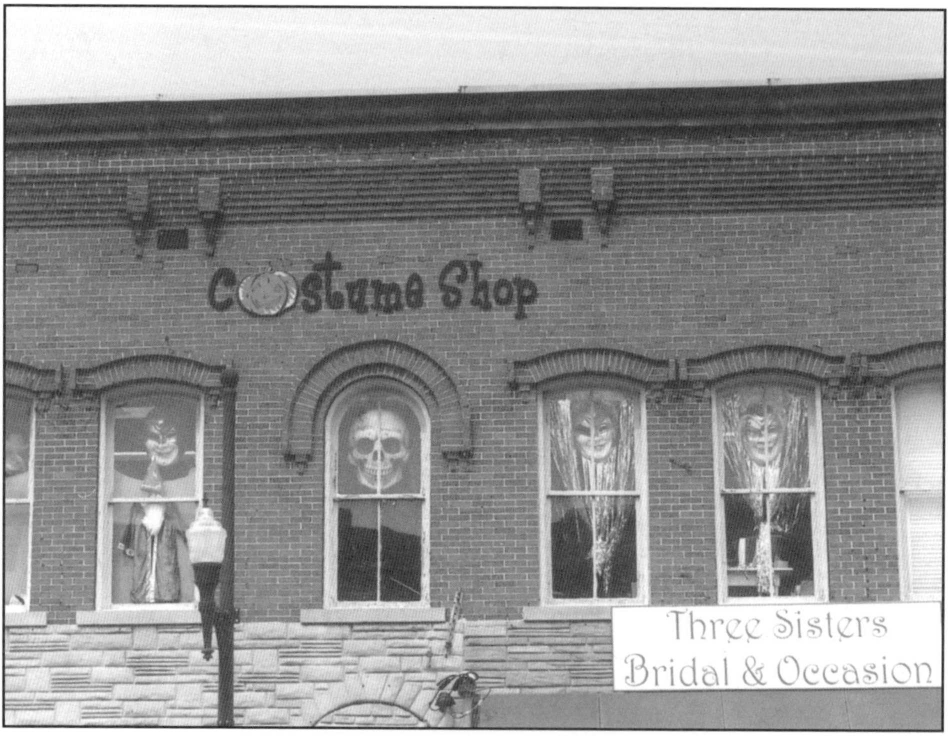

The Costume Shop, 2nd floor, Newnan.

Costume Shop
11 and one half Greenville Street
Newnan, Georgia
Telephone: 770-252-3202

When I started writing this book, I visited and inquired with every single business around the historic court square about possible ghostly activity. Many shook their heads, while others looked at me and laughed. But when I inquired at the Costume Shop on 11 ½ Greenville Street, they smiled.

Keith, the owner, said that while he and his wife hadn't seen or experienced anything unusual, the previous tenants did. He said, in fact, these previous tenants even came into the costume shop and asked him if he'd had difficulty with ghosts. He gave me the information necessary to contact the previous occupants. Keith said he felt they would be happy to talk with me. He added, from what they told him, they really saw and experienced some strange things.

I called and spoke with them and we arranged to meet at the Costume Shop. They wanted to show me around, point out the locations of the activity and such.

The Un-Private Bathroom

The first place they took me was into the bathroom. Apparently this was the place where the most frightening experiences took place. Certainly, I can understand that most of us consider the bathroom to be a place of solitary functionality. So when something invades that privacy, it is quite disturbing. This individual said that while using the restroom, he heard a knocking on the wall — three loud knocks, like a hand slapping the wall. Believing it to be a fellow co-worker playing a prank, he exited quickly, expecting to see someone in the adjacent room. However, no one was there.

Another instance occurred while he was using the facilities. He said that he felt something which had weight, but no mass, touch his shoulder area by his neck. Then, a patch of his hair stood straight up — only in one spot and near where he had felt something touch him.

He said, "It was the weirdest sensation. Almost as if someone was running their arm down around my neck."

They also told me about another occupant who heard footsteps, which approached, then stopped right outside the closed door of the bathroom. No one else was in the building at the time.

Fear of the Dark and Other Strange Occurrences

Both men felt a trepidation about spending any time in the building after dark. They were accustomed to writing things off as their imagination. However, this building proved otherwise. They agreed that the feeling they had reminded them of being a child and afraid of the dark — that strong fear, almost crippling. With the varied and persistent events, they could no longer brush the events aside so easily. We were also told that the current tenant's four-year-old child refused to spend time in the room, even during the day.

One time, the gentleman had his wife visit at the office. When she entered the building, she immediately stated that she didn't like it in the back corner. She said there was a very thick, weird feeling as they made their way toward that particular room. Many people have said that they also felt that way when they entered the building.

A gathering of friends went to the building after discussing some of the activity. They made dousing rods

and walked through the rooms. Many times the rods would cross, but they explained it away as electromagnetic energy fields and the like. However, in one particular corner the rods began to spin in circles, each one in opposite directions.

The building was old and the windows were in ill repair. So, to keep the rooms warmer, sheets were placed over the windows, particularly the room in the back right corner. A common occurrence would be for the sheet to blow up, straight in the air, as if a hard wind gusted. However, when they checked, the window was closed and no breezes blew outside.

One corner in particular of the back room seemed to be the precise spot of heightened activity. Both people agreed that the corner always emanated negative energy. During the interview, neither interviewee stood near that area long, if at all. Both men complained of that heavy feeling and headaches. Being the investigator I was, I took initiative and moved to conduct the remainder of the interview while standing in the corner.

The other interviewee told a story about when it was late at night in the fall. He was alone in the building and, he'd just finished painting the floor.

He said, "The heaviness in this room just fell. I just couldn't stay there any longer."

He closed the door, shut the lights off, and walked to the front of the building. There was a light on, so he turned around and went back to the light panel at the rear of the shop. He shut all the lights off and on before he finally was able to turn that one light off. It was completely dark, no lights what so ever. He exited the building and as he was

sitting in his car — which faced the front of the building — he noticed a different light on.

Up toward the middle of the building, they told me about a wall where they'd seen a shadow pass through frequently. They said it was a quick moving, shadowy image that would pass from one end of the wall, move along the wall, then disappear through the adjacent wall.

The men told me of an incident where another employee walked from the bathroom and passed the gentleman's office. She saw someone standing at the desk and said, "Are you ready?" as she walked by on her way to another office where they were convening for a meeting.

However, when she arrived at the meeting, two rooms away, the man was already there. She stopped in her tracks, mouth opened and speechless. She swore she had just seen someone — presumably him — at the desk.

History Hides the Truth

The only information we know about the history of the building is that it dates back to the late 1800s — around 1895 — and all of the original bricking and hardwood floors are still intact. At one time, the building served as a department store.

While we do not have any leads as to the identity of the spirit, one man believed it was a nurse from the civil war. He said he didn't think it was a harmful entity — actually, the opposite. He believed the spirit was acting just as she'd done in the Civil War — checking on everyone, protecting them.

Further Investigation…A Talkative Spirit

I used my digital voice recorder — as I do in every interview — to be certain I get all of the information correct. So later, when I went over the interview, I found I'd captured an EVP (electronic voice phenomena—see glossary), much to my surprise.

Remembering when the conversation took place, I could place where we were at that time. That particular conversation had taken place when I was standing in that corner. I reviewed it carefully, and sent it off to WGPS to review. They worked with it, pulled out all the sounds, separating them, playing the recording forward and backward. The male voice of the EVP has a very warped sound.

The voice enters the recording after the previous tenant said,

"I'm a Christian and I'm not supposed to believe in this stuff."

The EVP says,

"You'd better start . . ." and continues with two other inaudible words.

Another interesting event occurred when I went to take pictures. I went to the back of the building and the back room which seemed to have the most reports of activity. I set up my camera and started taking photos all around the room. When I went to photograph the corner, where I picked up the EVP, the camera would not snap the picture. I tried multiple times and, each time I pressed the button, nothing happened. When I moved to focus on another wall in the room, the camera took the picture without incident.

Chapter 5

The Family of Ghosts

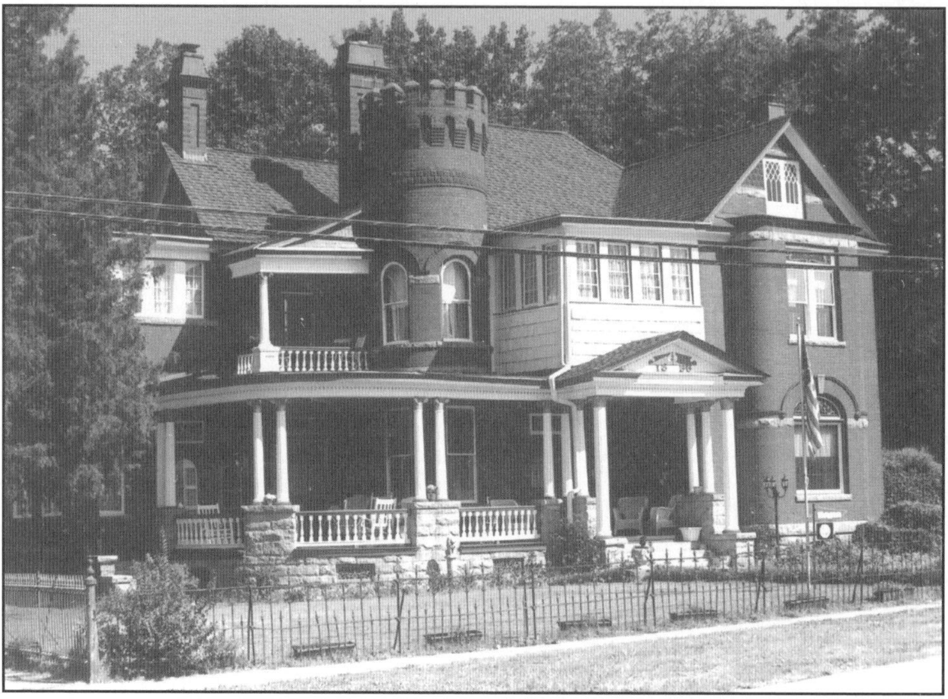

Two Post Street, Grantville.
Formerly known as Bonnie Castle.

2 Post Street
Grantville, Georgia

At Two Post Street in Grantville sits a beautiful, castle-like house, complete with turrets. Positioned to face the main street of Grantville, it's perched like a gentle guardian.

Built in 1896, for the J. W and Itura Colley Family, this Victorian home is on the National Register of Historic Places. The twenty-room mansion was constructed with local bricks, granite from Stone Mountain and heart pine floors.

Mr. Colley started the Grantville Hosiery Mill and eventually became a wealthy banker and land owner. Mrs. Itura Colley went by 'Miss Love'. She created her own business, selling handmade dolls known as Loveleigh Novelties.

A Bed-and-Breakfast Ghost Shows Itself

I spoke with the previous owners, who purchased the house in 1992, and operated a bed and breakfast there for several years.

He explained that many ghost-hunting groups had visited the home in the past. He could not recall the groups by name, but said that several different groups had come to research the house and cemetery area. Mentioning that the evidence these different groups could show were orbs, he explained that each group showed various orbs throughout the house and cemetery site.

They captured images of the orbs with varying mediums — both digital cameras as well as video cameras. The pictures showed the orbs moving across and all around. The orbs varied in size and intensity. Apparently, they would appear often and it was concluded that, in time, the investigators could recognize each orb time and time again. The orbs were consistent each time.

The first odd thing which happened to the owners occurred as they were midst their large renovation process. In general, there have been many reports of ghostly activity when renovations start. The theory is that with all the changes and removal of items, it causes the ghosts to come and keep a watchful eye over their property and all the activity.

The previous owner told me a story which occurred in one of the rooms, the one where the Colley's grandson once slept. They were working on the bathroom area, adding plumbing for a sink. The contractor said he felt someone standing behind him. He assumed it was the owner's wife.

Continuing to work, he felt a distinct presence of someone directly behind him. The presence remained, so he turned around to talk with her. No one was there.

Come and Play...

Another time, early on in their bed-and-breakfast venture, they had a guest who brought her young child with her. They were sitting on the steps when the little girl ran over to the stone fence and gate. The young child said she saw someone coming over to the property. She waved and greeted the visitor. Her mother asked her who she saw — since *she* didn't see anyone there. The child said she wanted the man to come and play with her. Her mother asked her to describe the man. The young girl said the man was wearing a wide-brimmed straw hat, light-colored shirt and suspenders. The mother never saw anything or anybody.

Musty Ghost and Light Shows

Once, the previous owners smelled a musty scent. It was very concentrated, and only in the breakfast room and bathroom.

"It smelled like a museum. You know that kind of smell..."

While the ghostly presence did not scare the guests, another time, a guest reported an unusual experience to the owners. The guest said she couldn't sleep because a light in the room kept her awake most of the night. The lights, she said, bounced around the room from ceiling to floor and all around.

A Pooch With An Attitude

And then there's the dog. The canine would never go into certain rooms alone. He'd only remain in the room, if the owners were with him. Perhaps he sensed something with his canine perceptions that we humans didn't.

Flying Figurines

One time, when the owner's wife had someone doing work in the dining area, an expensive knick-knack flew off the shelf. She said she was just standing there and her Hummel just flew off the shelf as if something had swept it off. It fell to the ground and broke.

She told the repairman, "You'd better hurry up," as she knew the spirit was apparently unhappy with the workman's presence.

A Cool Occurrence

There was a time prior to the interviewees purchasing the house, that several people would stay as night

Colley grave site, Grantville.

watchmen. One couple told a story about when they watched the unoccupied house. They said that while they were staying at the home, the air conditioner turned on. Ordinarily, that wouldn't be an odd situation, however, what frightened the couple was that there wasn't any power in the house.

Here, Kitty-Kitty

Another paranormal experience at the house was when a guest staying at the bed and breakfast asked about the cat.

He told the guest, "We don't have a cat."

They replied, "Oh, yes, it was at the top of the stairs."

Others have also seen the ghostly cat. It reportedly moved from the top of the stairs and walked down the halls. The previous owners never saw the cat.

A Night-Time Visitor

The previous owner's son — who was college aged at the time when they owned the house — would stay at the house during school breaks. He said that above his room was an attic. One night while he was lying in bed, he heard the small window in the attic open. Then he heard foot steps. He said at the time, the floor boards in that attic were not nailed down, so you would hear every step. The footsteps continued downstairs and stopped in the bathroom at the door to his room.

He said, "I heard like a dress swishing, but I didn't see it, because I had my eyes closed."

He told me that the swishing went over to the bathroom area, which had been newly renovated. Then the swishing noise stopped, as if the ghost was looking at the bathroom. It started again, and left the room. He told his mother about the strange event in the morning.

The Colley Graves

The cemetery up the street also seems to have a great deal of paranormal energy. Especially around the headstones of the Colley Family, as that is the primary burial site for the entire family line. The previous owners both told me that many of the ghost hunting groups who visited their home also found many orbs at the cemetery site.

The previous owners explained that they felt the ghosts were Mrs. Itura Colley or Miss Love and her daughter-in-law. Apparently, both women were ahead of their time and had dynamic, fiery personalities.

An Earlier Sighting!

A Newnan realtor talked to me about the house as well. He said he experienced some very odd happenings during a showing of the house many years ago when the Colley family first sold the home. This was before the other people I interviewed had purchased it for a bed and breakfast.

He prefaced the story with saying, "Now, I don't believe in ghosts. . ."

He told about a time when he ran an ad in the local papers about the house. There were several calls, and he went on a rainy Sunday afternoon to allow several different people inside to see the home.

Upon arriving at the house, he unlocked and opened the front door; there was a man standing on the stairs inside the house.

Taken by surprise, the real estate agent said, "Well, hi. How are you?"

The gentleman replied, "Oh, fine. I just flew in from Chicago to see the house."

The realtor said he was confused how this man was inside the house with the door still locked, but he went to turn on some lights, and left the man on the stairs.

He said when he came back to the front of the house, the man was gone, but there was an elderly woman sitting on the steps.

Again the real estate agent greeted the visitor. However, the woman then said she'd been sitting on the steps all day talking with Mrs. Colley.

He said, "Well, that's real interesting, because Mrs. Colley's been dead for years."

He then told me that he explained to the elderly woman that he was going to the back of the house to turn on more lights. He also told her if she had any questions about the house, to just ask and he'd be happy to help. When he came back up front, she too had disappeared.

That day they had several offers on the house and the real estate agent called the seller. He told the seller about the two strange people who were present when he opened the house, yet disappeared before he'd had a chance to talk with them.

After the realtor described them, the seller said, "You better sit down."

He explained that the elderly woman whom the realtor described, died before Mrs. Colley, and he had an uncle who was killed in a plane crash in Chicago who matched the other description.

The realtor told me the people didn't look strange, or transparent. He said they just looked normal.

He told me, "I always get chill bumps when I think about it. I really don't know where they went to or how they got in."

Further Investigation

I did find several reports online from either other ghost hunters or people who stayed at the bed and breakfast years ago. Pictures of orbs, taken during their investigation are posted as well.

The previous owners advise that the current owners do not wish to discuss the reports of paranormal activity within the home. The current owners have reportedly done a house cleansing. Please respect the

current owners' wishes and the fact that this is now private property.

Of course, the cemetery and the Colley family's headstones are still a place to explore the possibility of paranormal activity. An interesting event took place at the cemetery when I went to take photos. It was a hot sultry day, and I didn't relish standing in the hot sun, taking pictures. However, when I arrived in front of the Colley Family plot, a beautiful breeze kicked up. I remember thinking; I guess it's not such a bad day after all, as I snapped away.

That gentle, summer breeze remained constant while I wandered around the graveyard. However, just a few short minutes later, when I went down the road to the main part of town, the breeze ceased. I honestly hadn't thought much about it until sweat ran down my face. I realized there was no breeze as I photographed the Colley house, as the American Flag hung limp on the pole in front of the home. Perhaps the spirits were attempting to assist me that day, keeping a cool breeze upon me while I worked.

Chapter 6

Just Whistle Dixie

College Street at Temple Avenue
Newnan, Georgia

A Newnan Realtor, spoke with me about some of his experiences.

He said, "I've been showing homes, here in Newnan for many years. Honestly, I don't believe in ghosts, but I can tell you a couple of stories that are interesting."

The first was about a house on College Street which used to be part of the old College Temple Girls School from 1853-1889. During the Civil War, the school was used in part as a make-shift hospital — just as many of the buildings in Newnan were at the time — but the school remained opened during the war as well. Later, most of the buildings of the College Temple Girls School were torn down. However, two were converted to private residences.

A Soldier Waits...

His first experience with this house was the first time he listed the home on the market. He asked the owner at the time, "Is there anything we could tell people about the house?"

She said, "Yes, tell them there's a soldier ghost that walks up and down the hall at night and drags his boots. But he's very friendly as long as you whistle Dixie."

The realtor laughed and said he thought she must be joking. She continued and told him, "If you hear or see anything strange, just whistle Dixie and it will be alright."

He sold the house and a few years later was asked to resell the home. At that time, he asked the owners if they'd ever seen or heard the ghost. They told him yes, many times.

They said, "We'd just whistle Dixie and everything was fine."

Open-Door Policy

The realtor listed and sold this house many times over. One time, he was asked by another realtor, after Wednesday night church, to meet with him and to see the house.

The three-story house had a few attic spaces and a bathroom on the third floor. On their tour of the home, when they reached the top floor, all of the doors on that floor just opened. He said all three doors sprung open simultaneously.

He said he couldn't explain how it happened, it was just really odd.

Further Investigation

I would term this type of entity as a residual haunting, as it is one with repeated action of the entity walking the halls and surrendering his ghostly activity upon hearing Dixie. Although I've seen the house from the outside and have heard the story multiple times, I've not had the pleasure of seeing it first hand on the inside. I also do not believe a professional team has investigated this house.

Chapter 7

A New Home Haunting

Newnan Area

Many people assume because a building is old, it must be haunted, and conversely, others think because a building is new it couldn't have ghosts. These statements are simply not true.

Ghosts can be transient. If you have a ghost in your home and move to rid yourself of the spirit, don't be surprised if it follows you to the new house. Sometimes ghosts are connected to people, not the property.

Such is the case in my own home. We live in Newnan, in a new home, built five years ago. We are the first owners of the property. I never imagined we'd be sharing our home with a ghost. However, we do with several, and I believe I know one visitor's identity.

My grandmother was very special to me. We'd always had a connection. Two weeks before she died, I dreamt of her passing. She wasn't ill at the time, and there would have been no reason for me to have thought something could be wrong. When she died two weeks later, I told my family about the dream.

They said, "She came to you because of your connection."

Years passed and nothing strange or unusual happened.

Crash!

In the spring of 2006, I woke to a loud, crashing sound. I sat up and was about to go investigate when my husband convinced me to ignore it.

He said, "It's probably the cat."

I agreed and went back to sleep. The next morning, I worked in my office at home. Again, a loud crash interrupted me. This time, I was able to locate the exact direction of the noise. I knew it came from my kitchen.

I walked into the kitchen confronting the cat, "What are you doing?"

However, she was not in the kitchen. I found her, two rooms away, sound asleep. I went back to my kitchen and began searching for the source of the sound, thinking that perhaps my pots and pans had fallen inside the cabinets creating the loud sound. I opened every cabinet; nothing was out of place. When I turned around, I noticed my hanging fruit basket was swinging back and forth. That was when I wondered if I had just received a ghostly visitor.

I went back to my computer and tried to work again. I couldn't focus. Then I remembered my grandmother died in the spring. After a brief amount of digging, I found her obituary. My stomach felt like it fell to my feet and I shivered when I looked at the date. It was the exact day, only fourteen years earlier.

I grabbed my camera and took a few pictures in the kitchen. However, nothing unusual showed up on the film.

Since this had been the first and only time we suspected we had an encounter in our home, we eventually dismissed it.

…Not Over Yet…

Three months later we had two other unexplained events. My husband and I noticed the cat intensely focused on a crystal vase up on our bookshelf. When my husband went over, he noticed the vase was broken. He picked it up and showed me. The bottom was completely shattered. It looked as if someone had slammed it down. I had recently cleaned that shelf, and at that time, the vase was intact. Again, while we both thought it strange, we couldn't explain what happened.

The next night we were watching television in bed with the lights off. The light came on and we both looked in the direction of the door, expecting to see our daughter. No one was there. I got up and checked on our child who was sound asleep in her room.

As I climbed back into bed, a thought jumped into my mind.

I asked my husband, "What's today's date?"

When he told me, goose bumps rose up on my skin. Then I explained. It was my grandmother's birthday. We both wished her a *Happy Birthday* and went back to our television show.

A Happy Valentines Day? Or Not…

Another visitor came on Valentines Day night. I experienced something very odd. First of all, we keep our bedroom door slightly open for our cats to come and go. But the past few weeks, I'd had difficulty with the door. It had been opening in the middle of the night and waking me up because it thumped when it hit the wall. So it is opened with a force of some kind.

That night, it happened again. Both cats were asleep in our bed, so I knew it wasn't them. I decided that instead of fighting about keeping the door open or closed, I would just leave it wide open. I went back to sleep.

I was awoken twice by what felt like a palm on my chest. The first time, I thought it felt very odd, and wondered if I was dreaming, then went back to sleep. When it happened the second time, less than an hour later, I knew with certainty something had touched me. I also felt a breeze pass quickly through the room. I sat awake for a few minutes wrestling with the idea of a paranormal visitor, then went back to sleep.

An hour later, I was startled awake by what felt like someone sitting on the edge of my bed next to me. It really felt freaky and sent a very cold shiver across my side and my back.

I heard a male voice say, "Don't tell Mary."

I rolled over, since my back faced the side of the bed and then it felt like that same something moved and sat down by my feet. I was really tempted to turn on the light, but I didn't want to wake my husband, nor cause the spirit to leave. I also knew that turning on the light wouldn't help. After a few moments, it moved off the bed.

Again, I could tell it was not one of my cats — one was asleep and the other woke up and moved once the 'it' sat on the bed. This being was more than just feeling a presence. When it sat on my bed, it had weight.

The next night it touched me again. This time it was at exactly 3:00 am — and it tapped my foot, which hung out of the covers, three times. I sat up, put on the voice recorder and started asking questions. My husband happened to wake up when I did, so he heard the entire conversation.

First I said, "You have my attention."

Many times these types of entities are looking for recognition, nothing more.

Then I asked if it had a name and waited for a response.

I told it that the date was 2007, and asked if it remembered what the date was last in its world. I told it that, while I didn't mind it being here, its methods were a bit unsettling. Again, often these types of ghosts will leave, if you tell them they are unwanted.

I asked if there was anything it wanted to tell me. Then I said I was going to shut the recorder off. My husband spoke up and asked if he could give his input then told me about the dream he just had before he woke up. It was about a war vet. All the while, I watched the blinking red light on the recorder showing it was recording.

I shut off the recorder and went to sleep.

Further Investigation

When I downloaded the piece — it starts off with me saying:

"You have my attention."'

Then jumps to, "do you remember last…"

Then my voice interrupts and says, "This is to remind what you did…"

Followed by two whooshing sounds… They sounded like two gun shots echoing across a large empty field.

Then my husband's voice says "war vet" and talks about his dream.

There is an entire section of the recording missing!
I haven't had any visitations lately. Perhaps this ghost, a brief visitor to our home, heeded my warning and moved on.

Chapter 8

The Lady in White

Hutcheson Ferry Road. Facing West, Palmetto.

Hutcheson Ferry Road
Palmetto, Georgia

Along time Newnan resident talked with me about an experience he and his brother had in 1984. This burly young man recalled quite clearly all the details of that ghostly night.

It was two-thirty in the morning, and they were on their way home from a high school football game. He was driving and his brother was in the passenger seat. They were driving down Hutcheson Ferry road, from the Palmetto direction heading toward Roscoe. This is a very rural area. He said they'd just past Watkins Road, when they saw her.

He remembers, "Here it is, two-thirty in the morning and there's a woman walking along the side of the road. She's sort of hunched over and going the same direction we're going."

She was holding two bundles and he had the distinct feeling the bundles were children, babies.

When he went past, he slowed, searching for a place to turn around. There were no other places to turn around, except the radio tower on the other side of the road. Once he slowed and pulled into the tower's gravel space, his brother panicked.

"Please, don't turn this car around. Whatever you do, don't turn around," the brother begged.

He explained to his brother that this woman might need help or could be in trouble. "She was in her bed gown, a white flowing gown." Something must have happened to her. Perhaps her husband had done something wrong, and she was trying to get away.

He pulled the car into the tower's parking lot and told me that in the short time it took for him to turn around,

she had moved with lightening-fast speed and was now directly across from them.

Surprised, he said, "Whoa. Okay, how'd that happen?"

His brother saw the woman, directly across from them, and crawled onto the floor board of the front seat. He continued to beg his brother not to stop, to keep going.

The woman continued walking.

The interviewee instead rolled down his window to speak with the woman. "Ma'am, are you okay? Can we help you?"

She stopped and looked up.

He said, "When she looked up at me, brother, her eyes scared the *bejeebees* out of me…because I didn't see any eyes."

Where her eyes should have been, instead were just black holes, empty spaces.

Then, he said, his brother peered up over his shoulder and whispered, "She ain't got no feet."

Thinking there had to be an explanation for the lack of feet, the interviewee looked, expecting to see some tall grass which hid the lady's feet. That wasn't the case. There was no high grass, she simply had no feet.

He said she shifted her bundles and leaned closer to the car.

**Hutcheson Ferry Road,
Facing West, Palmetto**

Then she said, "It's okay. I'm going over here."

She pointed in the direction of the graveyard.

He said to her, "Well, okay. As long as you are all right."

He told me, by that point, he was more than willing to get out of there. He drove in the direction they had come from, towards Palmetto and needed to turn around again to resume their original course. He turned around, which took only a few seconds.

He said by the time they passed her again, she had moved over 300 yards.

I asked about her appearance. He told me she was entirely ash white except for her black eyes. She had long, flowing white hair and wore a white nightgown. He estimated her to be five feet tall.

The next Sunday, he told another long-time resident and older woman about what he saw.

The woman said, "You're not the only one who's seen her. She's been seen up and down Hutcheson Ferry for the last sixty years."

Further Investigation

I went in search of the Lady in White, driving down the long, desolate road. I brought my camera, as any good investigator does. I stopped at the exact locations described to me, as they were very easily found. However, when I stepped out of my car to take pictures, the camera refused to work. I found this odd, particularly since I'd used it to photograph just earlier that week. Each time I pressed the button, it wouldn't respond. I certainly had batteries, and it did appear that I had power to the camera. After several attempts, I gave up. I then took my camera to the

photo shop. After looking at it, they told me the lens was broken. Luckily, I had another lens.

I did go back, however, this time during the day to get the photos contained in this chapter. Coincidence or something more that my lens was broken? Perhaps I'll never know.

Chapter 9

Shackled to the Past

Poplar Road
Newnan

Many of the properties in southern Georgia had once been flourishing cotton plantations. In Coweta County, there is a particular plantation, located on Poplar Road in Newnan. I talked with a woman whose in-laws once owned the property and house. She told me, ghosts of the former slaves reportedly haunt the grounds.

Some of the large oak trees still have shackles which hang from their limbs. However, removing them is nearly impossible as vines have grown around, twisting and encompassing the rusty metal. It is a gruesome reminder of the past.

She said, "Many things would happen in the house like furniture being moved, doors being knocked on, strange voices being heard."

A Son's Friend

There was one ghost that continually appeared, but only to the children living in the house. It was an apparition of a young woman who would be doing chores and crying, while wandering from room to room. Typically referred to as a residual haunting, this apparition performed repeated activity with frequency.

However, the ghost seemed to focus on and affect the owner's youngest son. This ghost, as well as other spirits, continually visited him while he played on the grounds.

The woman told me, one day, the kids were playing on the lower level of the Antebellum home. It was late in the day and the sun was low in the sky. The house was somewhat dark, so the youngest boy went to turn on the lamp. However, by some odd circumstance, he was electrocuted. The other kids stood terrified and watched helplessly as the volts of electric shocked the little boy.

She told me, "The nanny had to knock him away from the lamp with a broom. They tried to revive the youngest boy to no avail. He died."

The mother fled the house distraught over her son's death. She felt thoroughly convinced that a spirit of the slaves, seeking revenge on the family, caused her son's death. She was terrified to go into or near the house after that day. The mother never returned to the house.

The family eventually sold the plantation. There have been several owners since.

...And Now One More...

Apparently, the home still experiences paranormal activity and, in addition to the other ghosts discussed previously, there seems to be another.

The most recent reports tell of the ghost of a little boy in the house. Common activity for this spirit includes turning lights on and off, and running up and down the stairs. Visitors and residents report that they hear someone knocking on the door, yet when they open it, no one is there.

Many have seen an apparition of the little boy and believe it is the child who was electrocuted. They say he's seen playing in the room in which he died that tragic death.

The Newnan woman told me, "My husband was talking with someone at a bar one night. They got to chatting, and the man told him that they just sold their house on Poplar Road. When my husband asked where it was located, the man at the bar told him the address and about some horrifying things which happened when they lived there." She swallowed hard before continuing. "That was when my husband realized that they were talking about the plantation house my husband's family used to own. The exact house where my husband's uncle was accidentally electrocuted decades before my husband was born."

Further Investigation

This house is particularly interesting since there are many reports of hauntings. Clearly, we can see there are two main types — residual and poltergeist activity — which has been present throughout the years and presumably, continues today. It is also fascinating to me that two distinct apparitions are seen — the woman cleaning and the little boy — within the same home. While I could visit the outside, I could not arrange for an interior tour.

The current owners do not wish to discuss the paranormal activity. No professional investigations that we are aware of have been conducted on the property. (Please respect owner privacy issues relating to this property.)

Chapter 10

The Screaming Bridge

Moreland, Georgia

There is a bridge located in Coweta County that spans over an old forgotten set of train tracks. Legend has it that there was a train wreck years ago which killed many people. It is said that there is a ghostly female apparition who wonders the train tracks at night crying and screaming her lost child's name.

A Real Haunt After All

When first told about this train bridge, I'd heard it was a hoax and fake. However, upon hearing this story, and confirming the events with several other people, it appears that it is indeed haunted.

A life long Coweta resident told me her story. She said, "The first time I went was with a bunch of friends while still in high school. Friends dared us to go out to the bridge and actually walk the same path the ghost lady walks at night. We were not allowed to take a flash light or any type of candle, lantern or anything because they said we would miss seeing the lady."

Others report the ghost as a very bright light. I asked about the description of what the ghost looks like, expecting them to describe an apparition. However, it seems the paranormal phenomenon is a very bright orb.

She laughed, then said, "Like an idiot, I went." Apparently, when you go down to the train tracks, you get the feeling that there is a presence. The area seems to radiate a certain sadness.

She continued the story. "Well, some of the group thought it would be fun to run off and leave a few of us standing there by ourselves in the pitch black night. While I was running I tripped and was separated from the group. Keep in mind I do not get scared very easily."

The remainder of the group moved in a different direction and she became lost in the encompassing darkness. Her friend, terrified as well, called out for her. She said she could hear someone calling her name, but it was very distant.

The Train! The Train!

She moved toward what she believed to be her friend calling for her, but before she could reach the others, a very loud vibrating sound started. It sounded like a train coming down the tracks. These tracks had been long out of use and forgotten.

The sound of the train ended with the sound of metal grating upon metal. At that point, she heard someone crying. It started out as a low sob and turned into a high-pitched screaming sound which lasted for several minutes. Then there was complete silence.

She said, "I was too stunned to move or even speak."

Nikki (her friend) was terrified and said, "Let's get the hell out of here!"

That was when the women saw a very bright glow coming from the end of the tracks. Nikki grabbed the interviewer's

arm and began pulling her down the tracks and away from the rapidly approaching light.

They ran as fast as they could and finally made their way back up to the road.

The woman told me after that night, she would no longer drive on that road, avoiding the area at all costs. It took her eleven years to go back near those tracks.

This ghost story has lasted for generations. And of course, was passed down to the many children of the county. Her son had heard about it from some of his friends. He asked repeatedly for her to take him to Screaming Bridge. Then, finally she got up enough courage and took him and a group of his friends to the bridge.

She took them right at dark and absolutely nothing happened.

The kids left disappointed, but she felt relieved.

Another Visit to Screaming Bridge

"However, one night when coming home from Six Flags, the kids talked me and my sister into taking them to Screaming Bridge," she said. Pausing to recall further details, she stated, "It was last summer."

They got to the bridge just after midnight and made their way down the hill and under the bridge. They did not hear what she referred to as the train wreck. (The train wreck she talked about was the grinding metal sound she had told me about earlier.)

They all heard the screaming and sobbing sound of the woman crying, though. Then they saw the bright light making its way down the tracks and directly toward them.

They all ran away — the kids scattering like rats — and back to the car. They never asked her again to take them back to Screaming Bridge.

She concluded, "I know a lot of grown men, my husband included, that would never do anything except cross that bridge in a big hurry."

Further Investigation

The area has been built up with houses. This makes the bridge seem less frightening, since it is no longer in the middle of nowhere.

Others recently reported going to Screaming Bridge, with no results. Again, we are looking at a residual haunting — repeated actions — and perhaps it is all a matter of timing. I did inquire if she could remember dates, but her best recollection was only that both episodes took place in the summer.

Chapter 11

The Lady in the Woods

Frances Shirey Way
Coweta County

The property owner told me her story. This woman and her family have lived at this location for several years and have had numerous unexplained events occur.

Long ago, The Shirey family owned the land. The property stretched for many miles and they used portions of it for farming. Reports indicated that there was an old cemetery on the land. The tale continues telling how the builders of the new subdivision, paid off the county commissioners (at the time) so that they would not have to remove the bodies.

This resident told me that several people in the area have found sections of what appears to be headstones. She had also heard that someone even dug up a small box which looked like a coffin.

The property owner said that her daughter, who was four years old at the time this book was written, has always been very adamant that a lady comes in and out of their house.

She said, "There have been many times when I have been alone at the house. I have heard someone walking

and called out thinking my family had arrived home. No one is there. There have also been times when I have been up at night, reading after the family has gone to bed, and I see movement out of the corner of my eye. I'll look up from my book thinking someone is standing there. Yet no one is."

She told me about one time when she was cleaning her house and suddenly felt a hand on her shoulder. She spun around, certain someone was there, but no one was.

Thumps in the Night

There was another paranormal event she spoke of. She said, "One night, it was just my daughter and I at home (the boys were at the deer camp). My daughter was asleep with me in my bed and I had just started to drift off. I heard a door in the house shut. I got up and started towards my bedroom door and that is when I heard foot steps downstairs."

She said she was frightened, but retrieved a weapon out of the closet. Then she went to check things out downstairs. That was when she heard a loud crashing sound. Terrified, she ran back to her bedroom, slamming the door shut. She locked the door and called the police. The loud crash had woken her daughter, but according to the woman, the child was surprisingly calm.

When the police arrived the woman went downstairs and let the officers into her house. They began a through search for a possible perpetrator. They found that her son's bedroom door had shut, even though she knew she had opened it just ten minutes before she went to lie down with her daughter in her bed. The police didn't find anything.

The next night, when she walked into her living room, she saw her daughter peaking through the blinds. She asked her daughter what she was looking at. The child said there was a lady in the woods waiting. The woman asked her daughter what the lady was waiting for. Her daughter told her the woman was waiting on her son. She immediately raised the blinds and looked out, but saw nothing.

That night the homeowner awoke, startled by her daughter who held her closely — almost nose to nose. The child said in a very odd, deep, and low voice, "The lady is still waiting in the woods, Mama." Then the child exited the bedroom and went back to her room. The mother sat awake for a while, pondering the very odd occurrence.

Twisted Tree

They recently cleared off some of the land due to a tornado which damaged some of the tress on the property. However, they found a tree which has grown around the strangest looking piece of wood. She told me several people have tried to figure out what the wood represents and how big it actually is. She said it is hard to tell because the tree has literally grown around the peculiar piece of wood, as if the tree made the wood a part of it.

She said, "My husband asked me if I wanted him to cut the tree down. For some reason I am compelled to leave it just the way it is."

With clearing the land, it was necessary that they burned the massive wood piles. One weekend they had a big fire going. They had friends over and everyone was outside by the large bon fire.

She said, "I looked around and did not see my daughter. I panicked and called out her name."

The daughter said, "I am right here, Mama."

The woman said, "We, my friend and I, walked towards my daughter and noticed she was standing by the strange tree."

The mother asked her daughter what she was doing. The child replied, "I am waiting with the lady in the woods."

Her friend, who knows the story of the strange happenings, looked at both of them and said, "It is time to go in."

They went inside, unnerved by the situation.

The property owners are convinced the odd tree needs to stay there. They feel it is somehow related to the ghostly lady, and it may help her find who or what she is waiting for.

Further Investigation

Sometimes children see things we adults miss completely. Maybe it is due to our constant habit of being busy. Too busy, perhaps, and we miss things.

Maybe children are just more in tune with the world around them, or perhaps they just have more of a connection with the paranormal. I believe this happens to be one of those cases.

(Please respect owner privacy issues related to this property.)

Chapter 12

A Boy Called George

Aspen Lake Drive East
Newnan, Georgia

Newnan resident, who I'll call Mrs. J, told me about a house owned by her parents on Aspen Lake Drive East. She advised of a mischievous little boy ghost that she has named 'George' who haunts the house. George likes to make noise. He will make a constant racket, which you can hear coming up from the basement of the house.

One time the noise was so loud, Mrs. J's mother was convinced someone was in the basement and she called the police. However the officers did not find anything.

Mrs. J said, "I spend the night with my mother any time my father is away. Whenever I do, I never get any sleep. George seems to act up whenever I am there. He either does not like me or he knows I am a mother and just wants to play."

One of George's favorite pranks is running up and down the front steps at night and continually pushing doors open and closed. He also loves to rearrange the pots and pans, causing a huge clattering sound. Apparently, anyone who has ever been in that house has heard or felt George in some way.

The last time Mrs. J stayed the night with her mom, she told me that George was in a very bad mood.

Mad As Hell and He's Not Taking It Anymore!

She said, "He appeared to be throwing a tantrum."

George trudged up and down the steps all night. Neither of the ladies would respond to his tirade. However, he became *very* angry when neither woman bothered to question if anyone was there at the door.

Mrs. J said, "I had just put my head on the pillow when he jumped on the foot of the bed! I was scared, but I sat up. I did not say anything. I just sat for a bit with George sitting on the foot of the bed. Then about an hour later, I laid my head back down and was awakened by something hitting my pillow."

Since she couldn't sleep, Mrs. J decided to go to the kitchen to get a drink. She sat reading her book until she started to get sleepy again. She placed her glass in the sink and turned out the light.

"I know the house very well and could walk it in my sleep in pitch-black dark. I was halfway across the kitchen, when I heard a growling sound coming from the corner by the table," Mrs. J said.

She said that when she was tired and ready to go to bed, she told him, "Okay, George I am tired and ready to go to sleep. If you are lonely you can sleep with me. If not, please go find somewhere else to sleep and leave me alone!"

Mrs. J told me that she went back to bed and a several minutes later felt the bed shift with the weight of someone lying down.

After some time had passed with no other movement or sound, she drifted off to sleep. She said she has not stayed over night at her mother's since then.

An interesting connection she spoke about was the lady in the woods. Apparently, both of these hauntings are from within the same subdivision. Mrs. J believes that George may be the spirit who the lady in the woods is waiting for.

Further Investigation

George appears to be a poltergeist. I find his method of garnering attention from the adults interesting. However, what I find more interesting is how he continues with his noise making until someone acknowledges his presence. Many other entities would have given up. Yet perhaps because he is a child, it explains why he is so insistent about receiving proper recognition. However, one point to remember with cases such as this, if you tell the ghost that you wish to be left alone, they will usually comply. I advised Ms. J to do so, in hopes she can be at peace in that house.

(Please respect owner privacy issues related to this property.)

Chapter 13

Into the Dark Alleyway

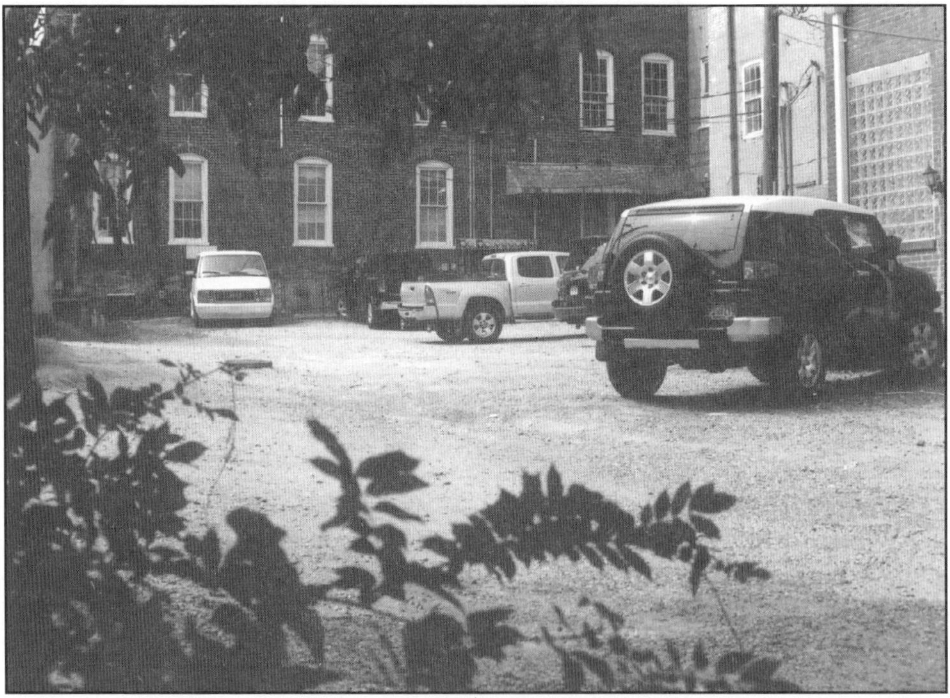

Parking Lot, corner of Madison and Jefferson, Newnan.

Madison Street
Newnan, Georgia

Behind the shopping and restaurants on Jefferson Street and facing Madison Street is a small gravel parking lot. This lot gives access into the rear entrance for the businesses on Jefferson Street on that block.

I heard this story a few years ago, but it stuck forever ingrained in my memory.

There was a fine-dining restaurant establishment in the heart of downtown Newnan on Jefferson Street.

The story relayed to me was about a waitress who left the restaurant late one night after her shift. After a few moments, she ran back into the building via the back door, with a look of sheer terror upon her face.

Several other restaurant staff listened as she told her story. She'd gone to her car and had her hand on the handle of the car door. Hearing something, she turned. Next to her stood a tall man wearing, as she put it, strange clothes and a hat. She said she didn't see his face clearly, due to the darkness, as there are no lights in the gravel parking lot.

The man asked her where she was going. As she started to answer him, he disappeared.

Several of the restaurant staff scoured the parking lot, looking for the strange man. They didn't find anyone.

From that night forward, the waitress always had someone walk her to her car after work if it was late at night.

I've heard other people tell the story as well. Some say he was wearing a Civil War Confederate uniform.

Further Investigation:

Of course, it is possible this entity is from the Civil War time period since the history of the town depicts Newnan as a hospital town at that time.

I believe this ghost to be an intelligent haunting, as he interacted with the young woman ,affecting the human world by asking her a question.

Several other reports about this ghost have been heard, however, many retailers in the area have never heard the story or seen the entity.

Chapter 14

Two for the Price of Admission

Front of Holliday, Dorsey, Fife house, Fayetteville.

The Holliday Dorsey Fife House and Museum
140 W. Lanier Avenue
Fayetteville, Georgia
www.hdfhouse.com

I had the pleasure of speaking with the museum's keeper, Mr. Lynch on one particularly dark and stormy morning — a perfectly chilling setting to listen to the tales. Mr. Lynch is a self-proclaimed skeptic, but happily told me about some of the strange things — as he put it — happening at the house. The Holliday Dorsey Fife house has a very intriguing past which only adds to the curiosity about the haunting.

The house was built in 1855 and owned by Doctor John Stiles Holliday, a prominent physician of his time in the Fayetteville area. His nephew, John Henry Holliday — the infamous 'Doc' Holliday of the Wild West — dearly loved his uncle and the family. Consequently, the house became endeared to the young Doc Holliday.

Doc Holliday is believed to be one of two ghosts who frequently appear at the house.

The Wild West?

One night, in the late 1990s, a police officer on routine patrol in the area, spotted someone in the right upstairs window of the house. The home was vacant and locked up tight at the time. The officer reported seeing a man wearing a duster staring at him. Of course, when a further investigation allowed entrance into the home, no one was there.

Mr. Lynch told me on two occasions he heard very loud crashing sounds. He said, "It sounded like a large mirror fell off the wall. It was that loud." When he went to seek out the source of the noise, he said he found nothing. Everything was in its proper place and nothing was broken.

He said that there are occasional noises and thumps, as well as items on shelves being relocated. He said that, one time, a replica cannon was pushed all the way to the very end of the shelf and was almost about to fall off.

Mr. Lynch also told me that the lights will turn on or off at bizarre times. He'll arrive in the morning to find the lights on when he knew he'd shut them off the night before.

He said, "There's no doubt there's strange acoustics in the house." He continued, "I'll hear someone coming up the back door landing. When I open the door, no one is there." He said that the sound somehow traveled throughout the house and he knows someone had to be on those steps, yet no one ever was.

Doors also open and close on their own at the Holliday Dorsey Fife House. The front door opens and no one is there. The attic door has an eerie habit of closing very slowly, but only when someone is standing in the hallway and watching.

Trapped on Halloween

One time, Mr. Lynch said, they had a very special Halloween event. A ghost storyteller came and hosted the event in the attic. At one time the attic held Doctor Holiday's medical skeleton, so it was naturally the perfect creepy place to host the event. When the storyteller was done, she went to exit the room. The attic door was locked. They couldn't get the door unlocked; it was stuck. Mr. Lynch and staff had to remove the door in order to rescue the trapped storyteller.

He said, "It never did that before. It was really strange."

A Murder...and a Ghost

I asked Mr. Lynch about his guess as to the identity of the ghostly spirit. He believes it is John 'Manny' Dorsey who died in the house. Reports say he was murdered.

Mr. Lynch's cousin took a photo of the house which revealed a shocking discovery. In the lower left hand window of the house was a man looking out. The man in that photo, taken in 1990, resembles another photo of Manny Dorsey which hangs as part of an historic display in the museum and was taken nearly one hundred years earlier.

Mr. Lynch said the spirits are friendly and do not mean any harm. He also said he's not afraid, but does think these occurrences are very strange.

Further Investigation

The Holliday Dorsey Fife house has had several professional ghost groups investigate. Mr. Lynch said that every one has found something indicating possible paranormal activity. One group had two equipment malfunctions — both relating to non-working equipment which had been checked just prior to entering the house. Another group reported that a voice recorder flew off of an investigator's belt during the investigation. And yet another group captured an EVP of a whispering sound which sounded like, "Get out."

There were several reports from a recent ghost investigation showing orbs. One photo showed an orb directly in front of Doc Holliday's picture which sits above the fireplace mantle.

West Georgia Paranormal, Joey Ward, shared his group's experience during an investigation. He said, "We'd set

up our equipment, then went with the curator to a near by graveyard. When we reviewed the tape later, we heard audible voices and what sounded like someone walking up or down the stairs." He also told me that they were certain no one was in the building, as they'd all left, locking the building and turning on the security system. Additionally, there were some pictures with orbs.

Chapter 15

A Woman Beyond Her Time

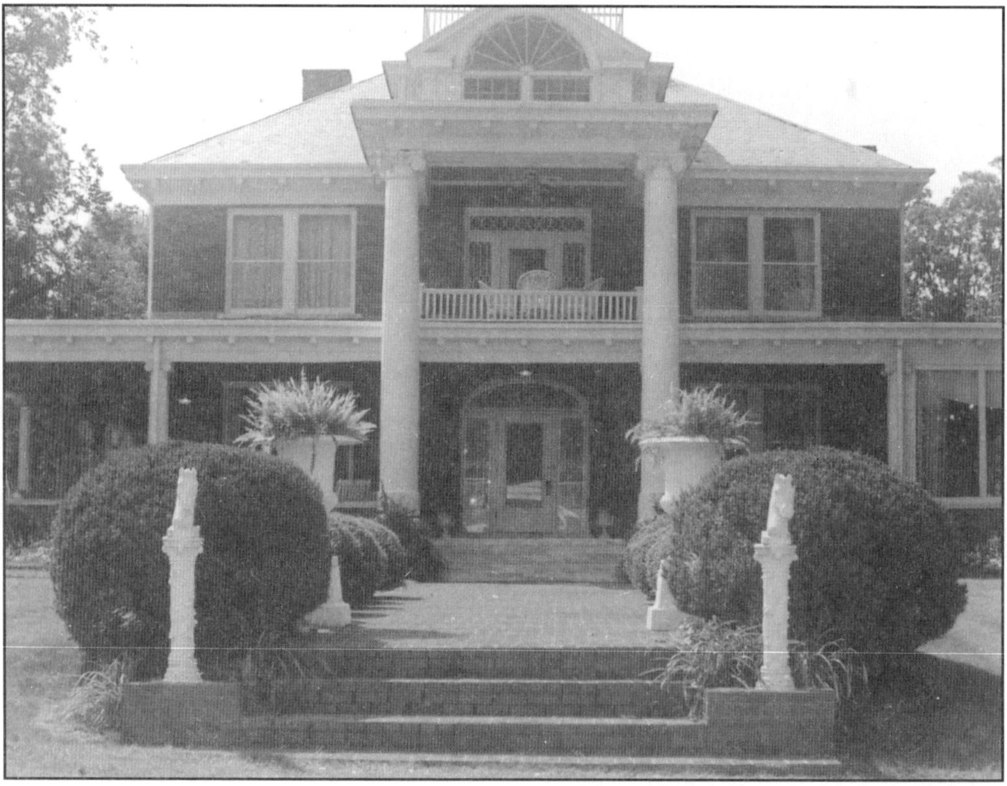

The Green Manor, Union City.

Green Manor
6400 Westbrook Street
Union City, Georgia
Telephone 770-964-4343

One very hot Georgia morning, I ventured in the sweltering heat and humidity to the Green Manor in Union City.

The impressive manor, built in 1910 has, as manager Ms. Linda Johnson tells, three ghosts who frequent the property.

The original property was given to Mr. Carmichael and Miss Westbrook as a wedding gift from the Westbrooks, in the early 1800s. The plantation consisted of thirty acres, and was home to the newlywed Carmichaels. In 1910, Mr. Drewry A. Carmichael decided to rebuild the house for his wife and four children. The new home, which is now the Green Manor Restaurant, was built with some very unique construction. Special bricks and white pine flooring was brought to construct the house. There are ten fireplaces, two staircases, and a large wraparound front porch.

In 1917, Mr. Carmichael sold the property to Dr. Green. He used the front room of the house for his patients and continued his practice until 1947. His wife, Barbara Green turned the house into a restaurant and managed it until her death in 1984. The house still remains in the Green family.

An Un-Lady-Like ghost

Ms. Johnson was very happy to talk to me. She said, while there are three ghosts, their main ghost they believe is Ms. Florence Westbrook.

Back in the early 1900s, a young and single family member, Ms. Florence Westbrook, arrived at the Carmichaels plantation. She acted as a nanny, assisting Ms. Cora Carmichael with their four children.

Ms. Florence Westbrook, a lady beyond her time.

Florence was a very rebellious woman by the standards of the time. She smoked, wore slacks, and rode a motorcycle. All of which was considered very un-lady like.

In 1914, Florence tragically died. She was bringing some water to the workers who were burning the cotton fields after the harvest, when the hem of her dress caught fire. She threw the pail and ran in the other direction, toward the house. However, she never made it to the house. She collapsed and died on the front lawn.

Ms. Linda Johnson said, "She's a very friendly spirit. She has never harmed anyone."

She said many people have seen Florence, who habitually appears in the upstairs left window or on the balcony. The left upstairs room, now a bride's room, was once Florence's bedroom.

Ms. Johnson told me, "We once put up new drapery treatments. Shortly afterward, as a local reporter was coming home, he saw something on the balcony. He realized it was Florence. She was pacing on the balcony. As soon as he came across the property, she was — 'poof' — gone." Obviously, Florence was very upset at the time, but has since become accustomed to the new drapes.

Another distinct sighting took place in 1996, when a police officer responded to the alarm at the restaurant. He had checked all the doors, and finding them locked, he walked around front. As the officer waved a flashlight around, he saw Florence standing in the bathroom window peering out at him. He later told people that when he saw her, the hair on his head stood up. Ms. Johnson said, "To this day, he can not tell that story without every hair on his arms standing up."

Gardens of the Green Manor, Union City.

Bride's room/Florence's room, Green Manor.

A Reflection of the Past

Ms. Johnson also said that, most of the time, you will not have a face-to-face meeting with Florence. While you may see her on the balcony or in her old room, the most common place is in the mirror. She said, "When you look into the mirror, you'll see Florence standing next to you."

One time, a group of nurses were at the restaurant on a Thursday evening. One lady went to the downstairs restroom, and upon her return to the table, called Ms. Johnson over.

The woman asked, "Do you have a ghost?"

Ms. Johnson responded, "Yeah, we have a ghost."

This nurse then explained how in the restroom, while using the mirror to fix her hair, she spotted Florence standing behind her. She said she turned around three times, yet while she could see a reflection of someone, no one was there.

Ms. Johnson also said, "Florence shows up in wedding photos all the time. Recently, one woman called, concerned because there was an extra being in her photo." The bride said that no one else was in that picture and had no clue how it could have happened.

Ms. Johnson told me another story that a bride had told her. The bride said that she was in the bridal room, nervous as could be and sick to her stomach. Suddenly, she felt a presence in the room and began to feel calm. The bride said after that she felt fine and no longer had the pre-wedding day jitters.

More Spirits

Another time, the alarm had sounded and the police were called to the house. Everything was locked tight, as usual. However, the one thing that set off the alarm was a hat. There is a room where a display of antique hats sits. Somehow, one of these hats was found in the hallway downstairs, triggering the motion sensor.

As for the other ghosts, well one they believe is the previous manager and long time owner, Ms. Barbara Green. One office employee said she believes Ms. Green's spirit sits in the office, watching everything going on. They all agree that Ms. Green, if it is her, is very pleased about the state of the business. Another report from

an employee tells about how they smelled Ms. Green's perfume. Apparently, Ms. Green would keep her purse in a particular closet and she wore a very distinct perfume. One evening an employee opened the closet and the scent of perfume wafted out.

The last spirit they tell me about is a man. They are unsure of his identity and found out about him through a professional ghost investigation. Ms. Johnson said, "This ghost group came in and were recording, you know asking questions and such, while in the upstairs bathroom." An EVP was caught. They told her that a man's voice said, "My name is not Florence."

Many times, the staff will arrive in the morning and the lights are already on. Ms. Johnson said that many men from the fire department, which used to be right down the street, would tell her how they saw lights on during the night, as they drove past on their way to a call.

Another interesting quirk to this beautiful manor, besides the ghosts, is that in the basement there is a hidden room. Ms. Johnson said, "We really don't know what that room was for."

Since this home was around during the Civil War, they believe the house may have been used as a make-shift hospital, as were many other homes of the time. Apparently, some Union soldiers accidentally brought to the house, were hung from the banister of the large staircase.

While they found many interesting things around the property, including a cannon ball, Ms. Johnson said to this day, they have never found Florence Westbrook's headstone.

Upstairs hallway, Green Manor.

Further Investigation

While I sat in the office, listening to the tales of Ms. Florence, a distinct chill ran across my arms. It passed quickly. While wandering around the mansion and snapping photos, I took every opportunity to view myself in all of the mirrors. Alas, I only saw my own reflection. As Ms. Linda Johnson will tell you, the ghost of Florence Westbrook will only appear when she wants to. Perhaps that day wasn't one of those times.

Upon talking with West Georgia Paranormal, Joey Ward told me he had a direct AVP experience here (Audio voice phenomena; he heard it with his own ears at the time it happened!). He said, "I was downstairs, near the front door, setting up the video camera. I heard a woman sigh, it sounded very close, right next to me. Like six inches from my head." Of course, he said, when he turned around, no one was there. He also reported that after reviewing their audio tapes, he heard that exact sigh three other times, taped from three other locations in the house — all upstairs.

Perhaps Florence was relieved someone was investigating her reported appearances, or she was simply bored by all of the undue activity of the human world.

A New Visitor

Upon another visit to The Green Manor, Ms. Johnson pulled me aside and told about another, very recent incident.

She said, "Last Sunday, Ms. Green's sons came to the restaurant for dinner." They were all standing in the hallway next to the large front staircase. "We were just talking and

a large gust of wind came right through here. It blew that chandelier around." The tremendous gust also blew the back door wide open.

She said, "Both boys felt a presence." Although she said the younger one felt certain the presence was their mother.

Chapter 16

A Few Extra Tenants

Poole Woods Drive and Long Oak Street
Grantville, Georgia

G rantville, Georgia is a typical small southern town. On any given day, you can go to Main Street and hear the salutations between neighbors and friends. There, you can sit in the park, under the shade of a large oak tree and watch as people shop in the row of retail stores.

Originally named Calico Corner in 1828, it was an early settlement under the newly established county seat of Coweta. In the late 1840s, and with the arrival of the railroad, Calico Corner grew. Calico Corner then became Grantville, named after Colonel L. P Grant, a railroad engineer.

I spoke with long time resident, Mr. Thompson who told me about two private residences that are haunted.

Woman, Child and Breathing

BJ, as he likes to be called, started by telling me about a residence on Poole Woods Drive. It was built in the 1900s, although BJ purchased it in 1983. He said he lived there for over twenty years. But during his first month there, in 1983, is when he first experienced the paranormal activity.

He said, "I was asleep one night and something woke me up. When I looked over, I saw a lady and a child standing in the room. I asked them what they wanted. And they didn't say anything."

BJ told me these two just looked at him, and he said after he blinked a few times, they just disappeared.

According to BJ, these apparitions were wearing turn-of-the century clothing.

BJ said, "They were both wearing these big, fluffy dresses."

He also said he could tell they were mother and daughter and that the child looked to be about ten or eleven years old.

This continued for his entire twenty year stint in this house, happening dozens of times.

Another strange incident BJ recalled, involved his dog.

He said his dog, Cujo, had a breathing problem and, at times, you could hear the laborious breathing of the pup. Nothing lasts forever, and Cujo died after a long and happy life with BJ and his wife. However, three months after Cujo's death, BJ heard something which startled him.

He said, "All of a sudden I heard him (the dog) breathing. I looked over at my wife and asked her if she heard it too." She had, and both agreed it was very odd.

Perhaps Cujo had returned to watch over his beloved family and home.

A Family Member Watches

The next house he spoke about was located on Long Oak Street. BJ and his wife came into possession of the house, when the previous owner, BJ's father in-law, passed away.

He said, "We see my father in-law all the time."

Sometimes they see him just standing, watching them. Other times, his father in-law appears as a reflection in the mirror.

BJ said although they ask the apparition questions, he's never answered.

Occasionally, they will also experience other paranormal activity. The bedroom lights will be on when they arrive home, although they know the lights were off when they left. BJ even went as far as calling an electrician, as he feared there was a short in the system somewhere. The electrician checked all the wiring and found nothing wrong.

Appearances in the Ghost World

Interested in the apparitions, I inquired as to the physical appearance of the three entities he spoke about.

BJ told me his ghosts appeared normal, almost human-like, not ethereal or transparent. He also said that he's not scared nor upset about the ghosts.

However, he did say, "Now if they started opening and closing doors or making a bunch of noise, then I'd be upset."

BJ told me he doesn't mind living with the ghosts. He said they just watch, and do nothing more. Perhaps these entities are just looking out for him and his family.

Chapter 17

Tall Tales

Every county has tall tales and The Southern Crescent in Georgia is no exception. I've compiled a short list and provided brief descriptions of stories I've heard. None of these tales were relayed to me by anyone who experienced or witnessed the activity. Perhaps they are just urban legends, or maybe they are more. But that is a tale for another day. . .

Newnan — Cedar Creek Bridge (Cry Baby Bridge)

The bridge over Cedar Creek on Roscoe Road is a replacement of the original bridge. In the 1930s a horrible accident on the bridge took the lives of a woman and her baby. The woman has manifested in voice and appearance in various ways over the last several decades. Hauntings include forlorn screaming (hence the name), rapidly dropping temperatures, and a ghost car.

Newnan — Manget-Brannon Theater for the Arts

Once a cotton warehouse, it was abandoned for years until the theater company inhabited it. Patrons and actors have felt a distinct presence, many of them collaborating on one particular area on the way to the bathroom. Several have believed the presence to be distinctively male. Reportedly, a psychic visited there and said she saw a man wearing a suit walk through one of the doors. She later saw him standing in a particular corner of the stage. They've blamed him with the many prop disappearances.

Fayette County — Old Hanging Ground (off of Padgett Road, near Starr's Mill)

This old hanging ground once belonged to old-man Padgett. During a routine hanging, one person broke loose, and in turn, hung Padgett from the nearby railroad bridge. It is said that old man Padgett still walks the tracks looking for his killer. The tracks have been abandoned for over fifteen years. Supposedly, you can still hear train horns and see figures on the dirt road and tracks. You can also hear voices in the surrounding woods.

Fayette — Woolsey Road Bridge

In the early 1920s, the sheriff of Woolsey killed many people and would dump their bodies into a swamp by his house. If you park by the bridge and walk to the edge of the swamp, it is said that you can see the ghosts of the people who were killed. They are carrying lanterns through the swamp.

Fairburn — Peter's Woods

There is an old cemetery in the woods that is reportedly haunted by an Amish girl. The story is that she was in love with a non-Amish boy and her father found out. He told her she could never see the boy again. Distraught, the girl went into the woods and hung herself. Sometimes, you see her ghost on the side of the road. If you stop to pick her up, she tells you to go to her house. Once you stop, you see her father run out of the house. He screams at her and she runs into the woods. If you chase after her, she leads you deep into the woods. You will feel something brush the top of your head and when you look up, you see her body hanging from a tree. If you look again, you see nothing but the remnants of an old house and a small family cemetery.

Newnan — Happy Valley Horror

Several reports indicated a Big Foot type monster was sighted on Happy Valley Road in Newnan. They saw two very large, hairy beings walking upright, along the road at night in this area. Reportedly, the Big Foot monster resides near water — possibly Lake Redwine — and eats armadillos.

Newnan — Belt Road Booger

The Belt Road Booger was first spotted in the late 1970s. The creature, described as a hairy monster which walked upright, ate plants from people's porches. They named the creature such, as it was commonly seen along Belt Road in western Coweta County. Reports of the creature flooded the police department and caught the attention of the local news for weeks.

Newnan — Old Newnan Hospital

People have reported feeling cold spots and having the feeling that someone was watching you. There have been reports by several patients and staff of a lady wearing white who makes rounds at the stroke of midnight.

Chapter 18

Ghostbusters, X-Files, and TAPS — Oh, My!

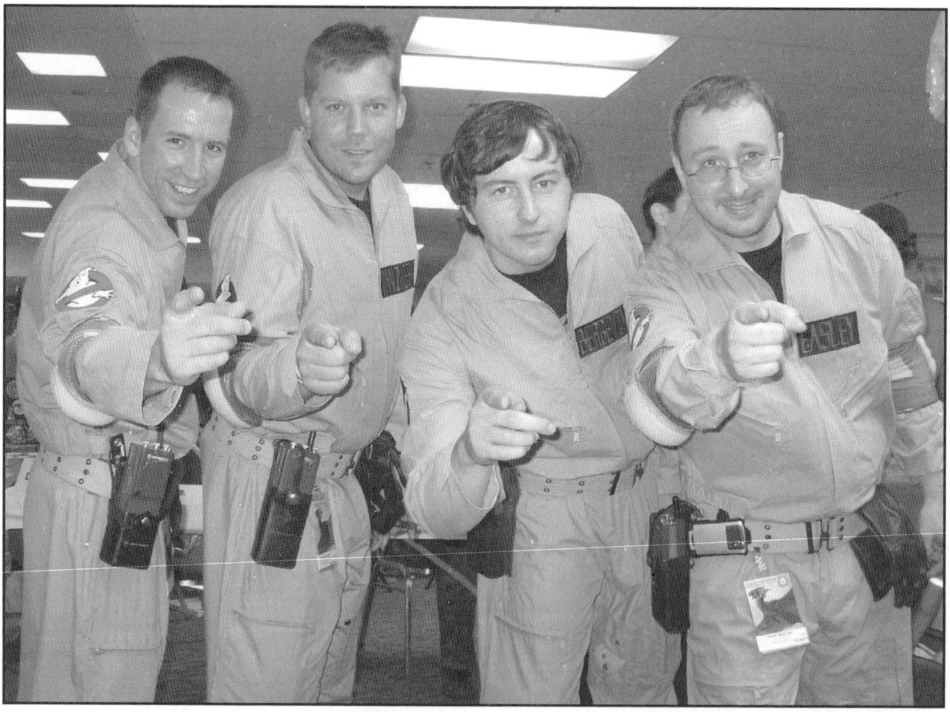

The *Ghostbusters* group at Dragon*Con.
From Left to Right: Robert Fuselier, Mike van Zwieten;
Joe Bergevin; Joel M. Easley. "Who ya gonna call?!"

Dragon*Con, 2007
Downtown, Atlanta

E very year over Labor Day Weekend, approximately forty thousand people converge at the Hilton, Hyatt and Marriott Hotels in downtown Atlanta. What do they go there for, you may ask? One word — Dragon*Con.

Dragon*Con is an annual science fiction and fan convention held in Atlanta, the south east's largest. There is everything from fan groups to costume contests, from vampires to movie stars, or creatures to ghosts and things that go bump in anybody's vision of night! Their programming consists of *Tracks*, with each interest area broken down into panels and activities within the programming tracks.

Of course you can find a plethora of informational panels on ghost hunting, led by the top professionals.

Interest in ghosts and the paranormal is on the rise. And in response to such an outpour of fan interest, conventions are ramping up their lineup by bringing in various professional ghost hunting groups, authors, and visually-appealing (or not) costumed creatures. But this is nothing new for the convention scene. With the popularity of television shows about ghosts and the media frenzy, conventions brought these *celebs* onboard just a few short years ago to provide another outlet for the fans.

There is definitely a fun side to the Con when it comes to fans of the ghost world and some of the media-driven excitement. It's been years since Dan Ackroyd, Bill Murray and the rest of the hilarious ghosty gang brought the movie screens alive with the *Ghostbusters* (and the sequels). But those characters are still live and well at Dragon*Con, and everyone who sees this creative grouping of young men,

know immediately who they are and what they represent! They're there for those of us who love the ghosts!

Panels or lectures are conducted throughout the weekend, ranging in topic from how to, to experiences the ghost groups share with the crowd. The professionals provide a ton of information and wisdom during the panels, and typically after the informative section, a *Q&A* session follows with the attendees able to pose questions to the hosts.

During the convention, time is set aside for these stars to sign autographs and talk one-on-one with the fans. I have to say that in 2007, the line for autographs from the TAPS group was the largest of the lines for the entire room — that included some very well known television and movie stars. The ghost hunting panels filled the massive space set aside for them — so much so they had to refuse admittance to some unfortunate folks who didn't get in line early enough. (And OH the lines...)

Dinah Roseberry, author of several ghost books and other science fiction and horror, was amazed at the number of like-minded people in the ghost world who routinely attend these kinds of conventions. This was her first Dragon*Con and her head was spinning with the number of activities and informational avenues to explore about ghostly phenomena. In particular, she attended a panel conducted by noted psychic Chip Coffey who told stories about the ghosts he'd encountered and other experiences in his hometown of Gwinnett County.

Seeing how actual psychics team up and interact with research-oriented ghost investigators was interesting.

She says, "Having a sixth or added sense that is measured by the human brain with actual details of the world beyond adds an interesting twist to the EMF/EVP evidence so often collected in ghost investigations. Then when historic accounts match the intuitive evidence, well, that's just cool.

But by and far the neatest thing about Dragon*Con was that every single person there (at least everyone I met) believed in the possibility of hauntings. That camaraderie makes a convention like this a safe haven for those who have questions or haunting issues—they can actually get a helping hand and sympathetic ear. Nobody is looking at anyone with raised eyes at Dragon*Con (well except for the guy dressed up like spaghetti... but even he was a hoot)."

While the panels conducted by professional ghost hunting teams are helpful, there are other benefits to attending. While you will get to hear the industry professionals (for example, TAPS) discuss their experiences and often disclose the how-to's of conducting your own ghost hunt, you also have ample opportunity to meet others.

Ghost enthusiasts of every variety attend the convention, as well as smaller or local ghost hunting groups. Perhaps you might need to find help for a pesky poltergeist you have in your home, or maybe you have captured an FBA (full-blown apparition) on film and would love to have someone with experience view the photo? Dragon*Con is a one-stop shop to handle all these needs! Or perhaps you just love the television series that highlight ghosts or just ghosts in general; at Dragon*Con, you'll feel right at home as there are many who just attend to see their favorite ghost television stars.

Others Have Jumped on the Ghost Wagon!

Many smaller conventions have also added paranormal guests to their lineup as well, so you don't have to travel to Dragon*Con to find a ghost hunting professional in your area. In the north Georgia area, several smaller conventions such as those noted below have ghost-hunting professionals on their lists:

Hallow Con — www.hallowcon.com
ConNooga — www.connooga.com

Check online sources, such as www.scificonventions.com or www.locusmag.com to find a convention in your area.

Conclusion

T he rich historical tapestry of Southern Crescent, Georgia, opens the door for imagination and excellent ghost hunting territory! Even the mere thought of strolling around Newnan Court Square with ghosts from the bygone eras brings a smile to my face and chills down my spine. Could a soldier from the Civil War be standing right next to me as I look at the time on the old court tower, or is a nurse following me as I walk into one of the fine shopping establishments of the twenty-first century along the Court Square?

Many of the stories contained within this book take place in public establishments, ripe for further investigation. Where noted, owners of restaurants and shops keepers are more than willing to talk with you about their buildings and experiences. However, please also note some stories take place in private residences and the owners wish to maintain their anonymity from the public eye.

Southern Crescent Georgia is filled with friendly faces, warm home-cooking, and a heap full of ghosts.

Whether you come for the unique historical southern buildings and charming, friendly people, or you come in search of ghosts, your visit to Coweta, Fayette, or Fulton Counties will not disappoint.

I hope you enjoyed reading this book as much as I've had writing it!

Wishing you—Unsettling reading,
Christina

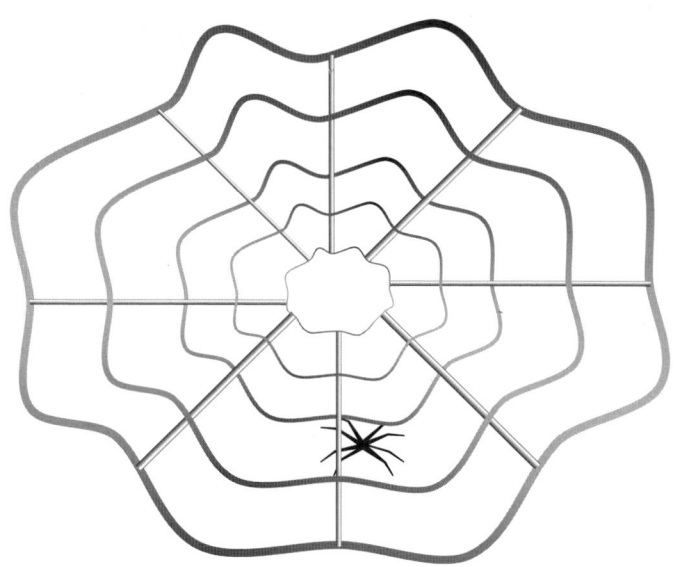

Happy hunting!

Top Ten Places to Find Ghosts

The following information is provided by author and ghost investigator, Fiona Broome and appears in her book, Ghosts of Austin, Texas. For more information, visit http://hollowhill.com/.

No matter where you are, certain locations are usually haunted. These sites don't always have ghosts, but they're the best places to start when you're looking for unreported visitors from beyond the grave.

Theatres

Ghosts frequent places where people have performed on stage. These include movie theatres that were once performance halls.

There are three kinds of ghosts at these locations:

First, at least one actor who is still seen on or near the stage.

Second, a stagehand lingers backstage, usually around the lighting or the curtain controls.

Finally, someone appears towards the back of the hall, especially during rehearsals. He or she almost always smokes a cigarette that people can smell, or they'll see the smoke or the burning ember.

Battlegrounds

Almost every battleground has some residual energy from the violent and tragic deaths that occurred there. Some battlegrounds are actually haunted by the spirits of the men and women who died there, too. Between Texas' battles for independence, Indian attacks, and Civil War conflicts, you'll find many locations with ghost stories... and real ghosts.

Cemeteries

It's a cliché but a true one: Ghosts haunt cemeteries. Modern graves—burials that occurred less than fifty years ago—are rarely haunted for very long.

For the most powerful hauntings, look for graves that are at least a hundred years old. Only a few are haunted, but you'll find elevated EMF levels at many of graves, especially if they're unmarked.

Colleges

Almost every college or university reports at least one ghost. Most also report poltergeist phenomena. The performing arts center is often the most haunted location on campus. In Austin, the University of Texas campus is probably the most haunted college.

Summer Camps

Most camps—especially Scout camps—have a ghost or two. Usually, these are benevolent ghosts of former camp counselors or the camp manager. An aroma of perfume or pipe smoke is usually reported, related to someone who worked there.

Very Old, Large Homes and Buildings

Like most ancient castles, many very old, large buildings have ghosts. In an older home, a woman who lived there lingers to be sure that the house and its occupants remain safe. She usually wears a green dress.

Another ghost is mad and lurks in the attic, basement, or an outbuilding. A variation on this is a ghost in the nearby woods or a field next to an old homestead. These hauntings are almost predictable.

Old Hotels

Many hotels are haunted by the same people who visited them in life. They're usually happy ghosts who return to relax and enjoy themselves.

Classic haunted spots in hotels include the top floor, the elevator, and the lobby. This is true of the Driskill Hotel, Austin's most haunted and elegant hotel, and a favorite destination for visiting ghost hunters.

Around Austin, this category of haunting extends to former brothels. In the late nineteenth century, dozens of feisty, independent-minded madams owned "boarding houses" around downtown Austin. Today, these sites are often clubs, bars, and restaurants in the entertainment and warehouse districts of Austin. And, most of them have great ghost stories to share.

Hospitals, Retirement Homes, Morgues and Funeral Parlors

As you'd expect, some people aren't willing to leave the last place where they were seen and called by name. However, if these sites are still in use, they're usually off-limits to ghost hunters.

Instead, look for former locations of these kinds of buildings. They're usually haunted by perplexed and sometimes angry ghosts.

Around Austin, there are probably hundreds of unreported ghosts. If you follow these suggestions, you'll find even more ghosts than are included in these pages.

Fiona's Tips
for Taking Great Ghost Photos

The following information is provided by author and ghost investigator, Fiona Broome and appears in her book, Ghosts of Austin, Texas. For more information, visit http://hollowhill.com/.

Avoid lens flares. Don't point the lens towards the sun, lights, a full moon, or any reflective surface. At least 80% of the orb photos that I review are clearly reflections from shiny surfaces or lights that are in the frame of the photo or just outside it.

Don't take pictures in high humidity or rain. Moisture in the air can result in dozens—even hundreds—of orbs in a single photo. If you see too many orbs in your pictures, or many very tiny orbs among larger ones, they're probably from rain or high humidity.

Watch out for bugs. Your ghost hunting companion should watch for insects in front of the camera as you take pictures.

Genuine orbs are almost perfectly round. If the orb is oval, irregularly shaped, or has blurry borders, it's probably an insect.

Avoid smoke. Tests show that smoke causes fewer eerie effects than most researchers guessed, smoke. However, even if you can't see or smell it when you're taking your photos—can cause misty figures.

Keep your camera strap and your hair out of the way.

Always take two photos in a row, moving as little as possible between the clicks of the camera's shutter. If your picture shows an actual anomaly, it will usually appear in only one photo. If it looks almost exactly the same (size, brightness, location) in both pictures, it's probably a reflection, or a hovering insect.

Save all of your pictures until you've seen at least a dozen with orbs and anomalies. Until you know what you're looking for, you may not realize how many anomalies are in your photos.

If you use a film camera, the photo lab may adjust the contrast to prevent the orbs (and other anomalies) from "spoiling" your photos. Sometimes, you have to study the negatives to find the orbs.

I've taken hundreds of photos that clearly show orbs on the negative but those same orbs are easily overlooked on the print. It took years of practice to spot these orbs without referring to the negatives.

When you realize how faint some orbs are, you'll probably find dozens of overlooked "ghosts" in your pictures.

Glossary

The following two sections are provided by the Chester County Paranormal Research Society in Pennsylvania and appears in training materials for new investigators. Please visit www.ChesterCountyprs. com for more information.

Air Probe Thermometer

A thermometer with an external probe that is capable of taking instant measurements of the air temperature.

Anomalous field

A field that can not be explained or ruled out by various possibilities, that can be a representation of spirit or paranormal energy present.

Apparition

A transparent form of a human or animal, a spirit.

Artificial field

A field that is caused by electrical outlets, appliances, etc.

Aural Enhancer

A listening device that enhances or amplifies audio signals. i.e., Orbitor Bionic Ear.

Automatic writing

The act of a spirit guiding a human agent in writing a message that is brought through by the spirit.

Base readings

The readings taken at the start of an investigation and are used as a means of comparing other readings taken later during the course of the investigation.

Demonic Haunting

A haunting that is caused by an inhuman or subhuman energy or spirit.

Dowsing Rods

A pair of L-shaped rods or a single Y-shaped rod, used to detect the presence of what the person using them is trying to find.

Electro-static generator

A device that electrically charges the air often used in paranormal investigations/research as a means to contribute to the materialization of paranormal or spiritual energy.

ELF

Extremely Low Frequency.

ELF Meter/EMF Meter

A device that measures electric and magnetic fields.

EMF

Electro Magnetic Field.

EVP
Electronic Voice Phenomena.

False positive
Something that is being interpreted as paranormal within a picture or video and is, in fact, a natural occurrence or defect of the equipment used.

Gamera
A 35mm film camera connected with a motion detector that is housed in a weather proof container and takes a picture when movement is detected. Made by Silver Creek Industries.

Geiger Counter
A device that measures gamma and x-ray radiation.

Infra Red
An invisible band of radiation at the lower end of the visible light spectrum. With wavelengths from 750 nm to 1 mm, infrared starts at the end of the microwave spectrum and ends at the beginning of visible light. Infrared transmission typically requires an unobstructed line of sight between transmitter and receiver. Widely used in most audio and video remote controls, infrared transmission is also used for wireless connections between computer devices and a variety of detectors.

Intelligent haunting
A haunting of a spirit or other entity that has the ability to interact with the living and do things that can make its presence known.

Milli-gauss

Unit of measurement, measures in 1000th of a gauss and is named for the famous German mathematician, Karl Gauss.

Orbs

Anomalous spherical shapes that appear on video and still photography.

Pendulum

A pointed item that is hung on the end of a string or chain and is used as a means of contacting spirits. An individual will hold the item and let it hang from the finger tips. The individual will ask questions aloud and the pendulum answers by moving.

Poltergeist haunting

A haunting that has two sides, but same kinds of activity in common. Violent outbursts of activity with doors and windows slamming shut, items being thrown across a room and things being knocked off of surfaces. Poltergeist hauntings are usually focused around a specific individual who resides or works at the location of the activity reported, and, in some cases, when the person is not present at the location, activity does not occur. A poltergeist haunting may be the cause of a human agent or spirit/energy that may be present at the location.

Portal

An opening in the realm of the paranormal that is a gateway between one dimension and the next. A passageway for spirits to come and go through. See also Vortex.

Residual haunting

A haunting that is an imprint of an event or person that plays itself out like a loop until the energy that causes it has burned itself out.

Scrying

The act of eliciting information with the use of a pendulum from spirits.

Table Tipping

A form of spirit communication, the act of a table being used as a form of contact. Individuals will sit around a table and lightly place there fingertips on the edge of the table and elicit contact with a spirit. The Spirit will respond by "tipping" or moving the table.

Talking Boards

A board used as a means of communicating with a spirit. Also known as a Quija™ Board.

Vortex

A place or situation regarded as drawing into its center all that surrounds it.

White Noise

A random noise signal that has the same sound energy level at all frequencies.

Equipment Explanations

I n this section, the Chester County Paranormal Research Society looks at the application and benefits of equipment used on investigations with greater detail. The equipment used for an investigation plays a vital role in the ability to collect objective evidence and helps to determine what *is* and *is not* paranormal activity. But a key point to be made here is: the investigator is the most important tool on any investigation. With that said, let us now take a look at the main pieces of equipment used during an investigation...

The Geiger Counter

The Geiger counter is device that measures radiation. A "Geiger counter" usually contains a metal tube with a thin metal wire along its middle. The space in between them is sealed off and filled with a suitable gas and with the wire at about +1000 volts relative to the tube.

An ion or electron penetrating the tube (or an electron knocked out of the wall by X-rays or gamma rays) tears electrons off atoms in the gas. Because of the high positive voltage of the central wire, those electrons are then attracted to it. They gain energy that collide with atoms and release more electrons, until the process snowballs into an "avalanche", producing an easily detectable

pulse of current. With a suitable filling gas, the flow of electricity stops by itself, or else the electrical circuitry can help stop it.

The instrument was called a "counter" because every particle passing it produced an identical pulse, allowing particles to be counted, usually electronically. But it did not tell anything about their identity or energy, except that they must have sufficient energy to penetrate the walls of the counter.

The Geiger counter is used in paranormal research to measure the background radiation at a location. The working theory in this field is that paranormal activity can effect the background radiation. In some cases, it will increase the radiation levels and in other cases it will decrease the levels.

Digital and 35mm Film Cameras

The camera is an imperative piece of equipment that enabled us to gather objective evidence during a case. Some of the best evidence presented from cases of paranormal activity over the years has been because of photographs taken. If you own your own digital camera or 35mm film camera, you need to be fully aware of what the cameras abilities and limitations are. Digital cameras have been at the center of great debate in the field of paranormal research over the years.

The earlier incarnations of digital cameras were full of inherent problems and notorious for creating "false positive" pictures. A "false positive" picture is a picture that has anomalous elements within the picture that are the result of a camera defect or other natural occurrence.

There are many pictures scattered about the internet that claim to be of true paranormal activity, but in fact they are "false positives." Orbs, defined as anomalous paranormal energy that can show up as balls of light or streaks in still photography or video, are the most controversial pictures of paranormal energy in the field. There are so many theories (good and bad) about the origin of orbs and what they are. Every picture in the CCPRS collection that has an orb—or orbs—are not presented in a way that state that they are absolutely paranormal of nature. I have yet to capture an orb photo that made me feel certain that in fact it is of a paranormal nature.

If you use your own camera, understand that your camera is vital. I encourage all members who own their own cameras to do research on the make and model of the camera and see what other consumers are saying about them. Does the manufacturer give any info regarding possible defects or design flaws with that particular model? Understanding your camera will help to rule out the possibility of interpreting a "false positive" for an authentic picture of paranormal activity.

Video Cameras

The video camera is also a fundamental tool in the investigation as another way for collecting objective evidence that can support the proof of paranormal activity. The video camera can be used in various ways during the investigation. It can be set on a tripod and left in a location where paranormal activity has been reported. It can also be used as a hand-held camera

and the investigator will take it with them during their walk through investigation as a means of documenting to hopefully capture anomalous activity on tape. Infra-Red technology has become a feature on most consumer level video cameras and depending on the manufacturer can be called "night shot" or "night alive." What this technology does is allow us to use the camera in zero light. Most cameras with this feature will add a green tint or haze to the camera when it is being used in this mode. A video camera with this ability holds great appeal to the paranormal investigator.

EMF/ELF Meters
EMF = Electro Magnetic Frequency
ELF = Extremely Low Frequency

What is an EMF/ELF meter? Good question. The EMF/ELF meter is a meter that measures Electric and Magnetic fields in an AC or DC current field. It measures in a unit of measurement called "milli-gauss," named for the famous German mathematician, Karl Gauss. Most meters will measure in a range of 1-5 or 1-10 milli-gauss. The reason that EMF meters are used in paranormal research is because of the theory that a spirit or paranormal energy can add to the energy field when it is materializing or is present in a location. The theory says that, typically, an energy that measures between 3-7 milli-gauss may be of a paranormal origin. This doesn't mean that an artificial field can't also measure within this range. That is why we take base readings and make maps notating where artificial

fields occur. The artificial fields are a direct result of electricity, i.e. wiring, appliances, light switches, electrical outlets, circuit breakers, high voltage power lines, sub-stations, etc.

The Earth emits a naturally occurring magnetic field all around us and has an effect on paranormal activity. Geo-magnetic storm activity can also have a great influence on paranormal activity. For more information on this kind of phenomena visit: www.noaa.sec.com.

There are many different types of EMF meters; and each one, although it measures with the same unit of measurement, may react differently. An EMF meter can range from anywhere to $12.00 to $1,000.00 or more depending on the quality and features that it has. Most meters are measuring the AC (alternating current, the type of fields created by man-made electricity) fields and some can measure DC (direct current-naturally occurring fields, batteries also fall into the category of DC) fields. The benefit of having a meter that can measure DC fields is that they will automatically filter out the artificial fields created by AC fields and can pick up more naturally occurring electro magnetic fields. Some of the higher-tech EMF meters are so sensitive that they can pick up the fields generated by living beings. The EMF meter was originally designed to measure the earth's magnetic fields and also to measure the fields created by electrical an artificial means.

There have been various studies over the years about the long term effects of individuals living in or near high fields. There has been much controversy as to whether or not long term exposure to high fields can lead to cancer. It has been proven though that no matter what, long term

exposure to high fields can be harmful to your health. The ability to locate these high fields within a private residence or business is vital to the investigation. We may offer suggestions to the client as to possible solutions for dealing with high fields. The wiring in a home or business can greatly affect the possibility of high fields. If the wiring is old and/or not shielded correctly, it can emit high fields that may affect the ability to correctly notate any anomalous fields that may be present.

Audio Recording Equipment

Audio recording equipment is used for conducting EVP (Electronic Voice Phenomena) research and experiments. What is an EVP? An EVP is a phenomenon where paranormal voices or sounds can be captured with audio recording devices. The theory is that the activity will imprint directly onto the device or tape, but has not been proven to be an absolute fact. The use of an external microphone is essential when conducting EVP experiments with analog recording equipment. The internal microphone on an analog tape recorder can pick up the background noise of the working parts within the tape recorder and can taint the evidence as a whole. Most digital recorders are quiet enough to use the internal microphone, but as a general rule of thumb, we do not use them. An external microphone will be used always. Another theory about EVP research is that an authentic EVP will happen within the range 250-400hz. This is a lower frequency range and isn't easily heard by the human ear, and the human voice does not emit in this range. EVP is rarely heard at the moment it happens—it is usually revealed during the playback and analysis portion of the investigation.

Thermometers

The use of a thermometer in an investigation goes without saying. This is how we monitor the temperature changes during the course of an investigation. CCPRS is currently using Digital thermometers with remote sensors as a way to set up a perimeter and to notate any changes in a stationary location of an investigation. The Air-probe thermometer can take "real time" readings that are instantly accurate. This is the more appropriate thermometer for measuring air temperature and "cold spots" that may be caused by the presence of paranormal phenomena. The IR Non-contact thermometer is the most misused thermometer in the field of paranormal research. CCPRS does not own or use IR Non-contact thermometers for this reason. The IR (infra-red) Non-contact thermometer is meant for measuring surface temperatures from a remote location. It shoots an infrared beam out to an object and bounces to the unit and gives the temperature reading. I have seen, first hand, investigators using this thermometer as a way to measure air temperature. NO, this is not correct! Enough said. In an email conversation that I have had with Grant Wilson from TAPS, he has said that, "Any change in temperature that can't be measured with your hand is not worth notating…"

Guide For Urban Exploration

The following was prepared by Scott Lefebvre, was written by and offered courtesy of Scott Lefebvre, author of Spooky Creepy Long Island.

I f you're anything like me, creepy looking abandoned buildings have an almost irresistible attraction as destinations for adventurous excursions.

Attractive destinations include abandoned buildings, usually the older the better, and especially asylums and churches, ex-military bases, and anything else interesting and off limits.

Many urban explorers bring back small souvenirs from their excursions. I still have two coffee mugs from the Ladd Center, which are precious to me. But I ask that if you do decide to visit someplace with the purpose of exploring it, that you avoid the urge to destroy or vandalize anything while you're there. Please think about preserving the site for other explorers. Vandalism only serves to increase security surveillance or make the site more likely to face destruction as a safety hazard and a popular destination for unwanted visitors. It's perfectly acceptable to take as many pictures as you desire, but the best souvenir will be your memory of the experience.

Things That You Might Want to Remember to Bring Along With You

Light

If your planned destination is a building, day or night, you'll want to bring a **flashlight**. If you enter an abandoned building, there will most likely be rooms that do not have direct access to the outside and will be dark without artificial light. It's also important to always be able to see where you're planning on going. The most common injuries for urban explorers are tripping over something underfoot because they weren't watching where they were going, or hitting their head or getting cut by something hanging down from overhead.

My favorite flashlight is the Mag-Lite mini. It's more expensive than the one-use flashlights that you can buy at the register or get for free as a promotional item with a pack of batteries, but it's infinitely more reliable and durable. It will survive a few accidental drops onto concrete floors, and the bulbs are cheap and replaceable. The light it throws is bright and clear and adjustable, and it's relatively cheap, so it won't be a big deal if you drop it someplace that you can't etasily retrieve it. It runs on double A's and gets pretty good battery life, but **make sure you bring spare batteries**. You don't want to be trapped in an unfamiliar, potentially dangerous environment with a handful of dead flashlight.

Photography

A **camera** with a good flash is also highly recommended. Digital cameras are lighter and often

cheaper than film cameras and can take a lot of pictures without requiring the user to play around with loading in a new roll of film in a dusty, musty environment. Plus, if you have to run, you don't want a bulky film camera with a flash attachment bumping around. Some of the most common sad stories about urban exploration are about broken or lost film cameras. Don't be one of those people.

Hair

Tying back long hair and wearing a baseball hat is recommended. You don't want your hair to accidentally get snagged on something and get pulled out. If you're going to hit your head on something it's better to get your hat knocked off than to get a rusty cut. Additionally, a stray hair flashed in front of a camera lens is frequently mistaken for evidence of the presence of the supernatural. A common and embarrassing error, and easily avoidable with a little precaution.

Attire

Wear **sensible shoes**. Sneakers with thick, skid-proof soles, or even better, work boots. The floors of abandoned buildings are often cluttered with debris and filth and sometimes damp or flooded. Also keep in mind that you may have to avoid wild animals or other hazards, so please be smart and tie your shoes. But only run if you're outside. Even a familiar spot might have changed since the last time you were there. Running in an unfamiliar environment is easily the best way to accidentally and possibly seriously hurt yourself while urban exploring.

You may want to bring light **work gloves**. Not so much to avoid leaving fingerprints, but more because abandoned buildings can be dirty places. There are rusty ladders and stairwell handrails and the walls are usually moldy. Anywhere you put your hands you can pick up dirt and you don't want that kind of dirt in your eyes or mouth. It's better to get your glove snagged on something sharp instead of cutting your hand open.

Just for Your Health

And speaking of mold and dust, if you're predisposed to allergies, you may want to invest in a good **dust mask**. In some old buildings there's lead paint dust and asbestos. I'm not too worried about breathing in a little toxic dust, but some of you may not be so careless.

The Legalities

Finally, as I've stated earlier, we all know that **trespassing is illegal**. If you're uncomfortable with possible legal involvement, there are many excellent places of supernatural interest that are perfectly legal to visit and explore.

It's important to keep in mind that even going onto property that is not public can be considered trespassing. If you enter an abandoned building, that can be considered illegal entry and trespassing. And if you had to do anything to a window or door to get into a building, it becomes breaking and entering.

On a final note, I implore you to not bring any **weapons** along with you while urban exploring. Having a small pocketknife or pocket multi-tool like a Swiss Army Knife or a Leatherman can be convenient and handy, especially

if your hair or clothes get snagged and you have to cut yourself loose. But it's completely unnecessary to bring a big hunting knife, or even worse, a handgun, along for the trip. If you're looking for ghosts, a weapon won't do you any good against them. Having a weapon just makes it that much more likely that someone will accidentally get hurt, and being discovered while urban exploring just gets more complicated if you're running around with a samurai sword.

Please be smart, be safe, and send me a set of your awesome pictures.

Or even better, take me along on your next trip.

𝕭ibliography

The Newnan-Coweta Historical Society. *History of Coweta County, Georgia*. Roswell, Georgia: W.H. Wolfe Assoc., 1988.

Jones, Mary G. and Reynolds, Lily. *Coweta County Chronicles for 100 Years*. Atlanta, Georgia: The Stein Printing Company, 1928.

Index of Places & Locations